FLAVORS
OF THE
SOUTHWEST

Robert Oser

Book Publishing Company
Summertown, Tennessee

Cover art by Kim Trainor
Cover design by Jeanne Kahan
Interior design by Warren C. Jefferson
Illustrations by Otis Maly, Kim Trainor, Warren C. Jefferson, and Dennis Caldwell

Printed in the United States by
Book Publishing Company
P.O. Box 99
Summertown, TN 38483

1-57067-049-8

Oser, Robert
        Flavors of the Southwest / Robert Oser.
            p.   cm.
        Includes index
        ISBN 1-57067-049-8
        1. Vegetarian cookery. 2. Cookery, American--Southwestern style.
    I. Title.
    TX837.075 1998
    641.5′636′0979--dc21   97-46068
                                            CIP

Calculations for the nutritional analyses in this book are based on the average number of servings listed with the recipes and the average amount of an ingredient if a range is called for. Calculations are rounded up to the nearest gram. If two options for an ingredient are listed, the first one is used. Not included are fat used for frying, unless the amount is specified in the recipe, optional ingredients, or serving suggestions.

CONTENTS

INTRODUCTION

Southwestern cuisine is often confused with Mexican cooking, and to be sure, there are many shared ingredients or dishes. The origin or base of both cuisines is Native American. In the southwestern United States, early cooks relied to a large extent on what is known in Native American tradition as the "three sisters": corn, beans, and squash.

Spanish culture brought with it traditional Spanish dishes that were soon adapted to new ingredients found in the area. New plants and agricultural techniques were also introduced to the area and combined with the three sisters to create new dishes. To the corn, beans, and squash were added chiles, cilantro, tomatoes, and rice. Other settlers—from Germany, Ireland, Italy, and other corners of the globe—added their native dishes to the local cuisine. And, of course, each region of the Southwest began to develop their own local dishes also, resulting in subtle but noticeable differences between, say, the cuisine of New Mexico and the cuisine of Texas (or what has come to be known as Tex-Mex). In Tucson, where I lived recently, the cuisine is known as Sonoran because of its origin in the Sonoran desert of Mexico. Because California is a connecting point for much of the world, Southwestern dishes from that region take on a much more eclectic, experimental flavor, combining more exotic ingredients from other cultures and influences.

There is, then, a continuing revolution in eating and cooking in the Southwest. Much of it is based on old techniques, updated to fit contemporary needs, and ingredients that are rooted in the history of another culture and place. As with cuisine everywhere, the art of cooking is not static, but constantly changing and evolving.

Contemporary Southwestern cuisine embodies the best of this evolution. Especially now, we see influences from various other cultures and ethnic origins—tofu and tempeh, sauerkraut, shiitake and portobello mushrooms, sundried tomatoes, seitan, balsamic vinegar, and the like—being incorporated into or substituted for other, more traditional ingredients. They retain the basic flavor and "spirit" of the dish, but it becomes even more exciting as we break down the limits of how we define Southwestern cuisine, expanding the basic foundation of Spanish and Native influences to include the rest of the "global community."

Creativity and the Art of Cooking

You are only limited by your imagination. Imagine! No limits!

—Baba Bob

Although I grew up in the Midwest, we were fortunate to have a Mexican community nearby which offered "authentic Mexican cuisine," so at a very young age I learned the difference between what Mexican food was supposed to taste like and the homogenized, tasteless versions offered at fast food franchises. I began to experiment at home, having "fiestas" and making large pots of chili and taco meat, always with a large skillet of frijoles (refried beans). As the world began to shift from an animal-based diet to one of mostly plant foods, I started experimenting with making chili and tacos using soy products and substituting for the meat used in traditional recipes. Soon I was serving vegetarian Mexican foods to my friends, and, generally, only those who knew I had given up meat thought to question what was in the new dishes. Most people couldn't tell the difference.

Please keep in mind, and I want to emphasize this, that the recipes in this (and ALL) cookbooks are suggestions. They are not carved in stone. I urge readers to change the recipes to fit their own needs, personalize them as to taste, nutritional and health needs, and availability of ingredients. Creativity is, I feel, the soul of good cooking. One of my personal goals in writing this cookbook is to help cooks tap into that source of creativity. That is why there are suggestions and variations following many of the recipes. Several of the quotes and cooking tips are also intended to give the cook a little push, to take that leap of faith necessary to create something new and exciting. I would enjoy nothing more than to receive letters that tell me, "I have made several of the recipes from your book and have changed several ingredients in each, substituting this for that, more spice, less fat, in fact, I changed the entire recipe, and it came out great!"

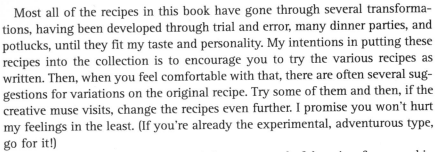

Most all of the recipes in this book have gone through several transformations, having been developed through trial and error, many dinner parties, and potlucks, until they fit my taste and personality. My intentions in putting these recipes into the collection is to encourage you to try the various recipes as written. Then, when you feel comfortable with that, there are often several suggestions for variations on the original recipe. Try some of them and then, if the creative muse visits, change the recipes even further. I promise you won't hurt my feelings in the least. (If you're already the experimental, adventurous type, go for it!)

A few years ago someone handed me a wonderful recipe for pumpkin soup. The interesting thing about this particular recipe is that there was a list of ingredients for the soup, but then there were four different sets of instructions on how to make it, each according to the four basic personality types described in the Meyer-Briggs personality test. For example, one type of personality is very precise and exact. The directions for this personality type called for having measuring utensils handy—not just measuring cups and spoons, but also scales, calipers, tape measure, etc. Another cooking style (the one matching my own) called for no measuring utensils at all (go by what you think will work) and stated to the effect, "since you're going to be making pumpkin soup, you might want to use pumpkin, but, if you prefer, you might substitute carrots, butternut squash, or something else orange, but you can use other vegetables, if you like, for a green soup, or whatever color you want."

Far be it from me to think I can or should change anyone's personality, but I do believe there are many cooks (and eaters) who would like to loosen up a bit but lack the confidence to try something different. I believe that confidence comes with experience. If you feel the urge to substitute an ingredient, add or decrease, or even eliminate an ingredient, or change the recipe radically—do it! (It might be a good idea, however, to save your most radical experiments for those times when you are not having the boss or in-laws to dinner—save it for another time.) If it doesn't work out, don't become discouraged. Think of what you liked or didn't like about the dish and how you would change it the next time to bring it closer to the dish you envision it could be.

To me, then, cooking is an art rather than a science, and as art it is growing, evolving, and changing. There are some techniques and basics in cooking that have been proven to be effective in getting a certain result, but other than that, nothing is sacred.

You will notice that some recipes may call for eggs or cheese, but I always try to give substitutions so that all of the dishes in this book may be made completely vegan, if desired. It is not my desire to push any particular diet or dietary philosophy other than the general belief that less-processed, natural, organic foods will be more nutritious, tastier, and, in the long run, less expensive. I see no reason to include meat or lard in the recipes (and lots of reasons not to), so they are not used. The debate about whether animal-based foods such as cheese, butter, or milk are more or less desirable than soy cheese, margarine, soymilk, or rice milk will go on for a while, and I'll leave that choice up to the individual. If you do use dairy products, buy only organic or from sources that do not use growth hormones and antibiotics. All of the recipes in this book can be made using dairy products or substituting soy- or rice-based milks and cheeses. Soymilk, rice milk, almond milk, and oat milk are all available in many natural foods stores and co-ops and substitute quite well for cows' milk. There are also varieties of soy, rice, and almond cheese on the market. If you are avoiding animal products altogether, be aware that most soy cheeses contain casein, a milk protein that allows the cheese to melt well. There are a few vegan cheeses available if you want to avoid casein.

Personally, I try to avoid animal products as much as possible with the following exceptions: I do use small amounts of organic butter and cheeses. I consider hydrogenated margarine a definite health hazard. I tend to use vegetable oils in place of either margarine or butter wherever possible, but if I must choose between margarine or butter for a dish, I will opt for a small amount of butter.

Please, then, experiment! Discover new ingredients, techniques, and dishes! Create you own! How about a mango-brie quesadilla with scallions and mint leaves? Why not a little pineapple in the chili? Above all, enjoy!

In the beginner's mind there are many possibilities; in the expert's mind are few.
-Shunryu Suzuki

TRADITIONAL FLAVORS OF THE SOUTHWEST

Beans

Beans are not only delicious and versatile, they are also a wonderful source of vitamins A and C, the B vitamins, calcium, phosphorus, potassium, and iron. One cup of cooked beans contains 5 to 7 grams of usable protein and less than 1 gram of fat (except soybeans, which have 15 grams of fat per 1 cup serving). Beans are also a good source of fiber, and their protein content makes them an excellent alternative to meat (which, by the way, has no fiber).

When buying beans, remember that 1 pound of dry beans equals about 2 cups and yields 6 cups of cooked beans. Dried beans will keep up to a year if stored in an airtight container at room temperature.

Adzuki (azuki, aduki, adsuki): Adzukis, native to the Orient, are a small, oval, burgundy-colored bean with a white stripe. They are easy to digest and have a delicate, sweet flavor and soft texture. Use them in soups, salads, stir-fries, bean cakes, and pasta dishes. Adzukis combine well with winter squash, sweet red pepper, and brown rice and are delicious seasoned with tamari, ginger, or Chinese 5-spice seasoning. Open kettle cooking time: 1 hour. Pressure cooking time: soaked beans 15 minutes, unsoaked beans 20 minutes.

Anasazi: A red and white speckled bean originally cultivated by Native Americans, anasazi beans lose their mottled appearance during cooking. They have a size and shape similar to pinto beans and are sweet, full flavored, and have a mealy texture. Anasazis are excellent in Mexican dishes, such as refried beans, burritos, and bean dips, and they combine well with tomatoes, corn, squash, and peppers. Season with garlic, chiles, cilantro, cumin, or coriander. Open kettle cooking time: 1 hour. Pressure cooking time: soaked beans 20 minutes, unsoaked beans 25 minutes.

Black (turtle): These small, round, purple-black beans are a staple of Latin America and the Orient. They have a distinct, earthy flavor and mealy texture and are excellent in Mexican, Caribbean, and Southwestern dishes, such as sauces, soups, bean cakes, refried beans, salads, and bean dips. Black beans combine well with tomatoes, corn, avocados, rice, and other grains. Season with garlic, lime juice, chiles, cardamom, cumin, or fresh cilantro. Open kettle cooking time: 1½ hours. Pressure cooking time: soaked beans 15 minutes, unsoaked beans 20 minutes.

Chick-peas (garbanzo): These medium-sized, round, tan beans have a nut-like flavor and firm texture and are popular in Middle Eastern and Mediterranean cooking. Chick-peas are often used in dips (such as hummus), soups, salads, croquettes (falafel), curries, and pasta dishes. They combine well with couscous, winter squash and yams, and eggplant. Season with olive oil, garlic, lemon juice, parsley, rosemary, mint, or cardamom. Open kettle cooking time: 1½ to 2 hours. Pressure cooking time: soaked beans 20 minutes, unsoaked beans 30 minutes.

Cranberry: These pink and beige mottled beans are related to kidney beans. Their colors fade during cooking, and they have an earthy flavor and mealy texture. Use cranberry beans in soups, stews, bean cakes, refried beans, and casseroles. They combine well with chiles, corn, and squash. Season with garlic or rosemary. Open kettle cooking time: 1 to 1½ hours. Pressure cooking time: soaked beans 20 minutes, unsoaked beans 25 minutes.

Fava (broad): These large, flat, kidney-shaped brown beans have a strong, almost bitter flavor and granular texture. They are popular in the Middle East and Italy in dishes such as soups, stews, and casseroles. They combine well with tomatoes, sweet bell peppers, and dairy or soy Parmesan cheese. Season with garlic, chiles, and cumin. Open kettle cooking time: 1 to 1½ hours. Pressure cooking time: soaked beans 20 minutes, unsoaked beans 25 minutes.

Kidney: These are relatively large beans and are most often used in chilis and bean salads. You can substitute kidney beans for pintos in frijoles. They combine well with chiles, onions, tomatoes, squash, and corn. I often like to use kidney beans mixed with pinto and black turtle beans for a colorful trio. Season with garlic, epazote, cumin, cilantro, and oregano. Open kettle cooking time: 1½ hours. Pressure cooking time: soaked beans 20 minutes, unsoaked beans 25 minutes.

Lentil: These small, disk-shaped seeds may be yellow, red, green, or brown. Enjoy their delicate, earthy flavor and creamy texture in soups, salads, purées, dips, pâtés, burgers, and curries. Lentils combine well with most vegetables and grains. Season with garlic, onion, thyme, curry, oregano, and parsley. Open kettle cooking time: 30 to 40 minutes. Pressure cooking time: 10 to 12 minutes. Soaking is not required for either cooking method.

Mung: These small, oblong, dark olive beans are native to India. They have a delicate, sweet flavor and soft texture and are easy to digest. Mung beans combine well with rice and vegetables. Season with tamari or ginger. Open kettle cooking time: 45 minutes. Pressure cooking time: 20 minutes. Soaking is not required for either method.

Pinto: These oval, pink and brown speckled beans are native to Mexico. Their color fades to brown during cooking, and they have a full-bodied, earthy flavor and mealy texture. Pintos are great for Tex-Mex dishes, where they are commonly used in refried beans and chili. They combine well with onions, tomatoes, squash, and corn. Season with garlic, chiles, cumin, and cilantro. Open kettle cooking time: 1½ hours. Pressure cooking time: soaked beans 20 minutes, unsoaked beans 25 minutes.

Rattlesnake: These dark, reddish brown, mottled beans are similar to pintos, with an earthy flavor and mealy texture. Rattlesnake beans are great for Tex-Mex, Mexican, or Southwestern cuisine, especially refried beans, chili, stews, soups, and casseroles. They combine well with chiles, onions, tomatoes, squash, and corn. Season with garlic, epazote, cumin, cilantro, and oregano. Open kettle cooking time: 1½ hours. Pressure cooking time: soaked beans 20 minutes, unsoaked beans 25 minutes.

Small red (Mexican red): These dark red beans are similar to kidney beans, only smaller. They have a rich, sweet flavor, mealy texture, and hold their shape during cooking. Most often used in soups, salads, chili, refried beans, and Creole dishes, small red beans combine well with tomatoes, corn, and summer squash. Substitute them for kidney or pinto beans in any recipe. Season with garlic, onion, chiles, cumin, and cilantro. Open kettle cooking time: 1 to 1½ hours. Pressure cooking time: soaked beans 20 minutes, unsoaked beans 25 minutes.

Soy: These pea-shaped beans, native to Central China, may be yellow, green, brown, or black. They have a mild, nutty flavor and firm texture.

Soybeans are commonly used to make tofu, tempeh, and tamari and are also are great in soups, stews, salads, burgers, and baked beans. Season with garlic, ginger, and tamari. Open kettle cooking is not recommended. Pressure cooking time: soaked beans 45 minutes, unsoaked beans 1 hour.

Tepary: These small, kidney-shaped beans are native to the southwest U.S. They may be white or brown and have an earthy, nutty flavor and firm texture. Tepary beans are used for refried beans and chili and combine well with onions, tomatoes, corn, and squash. Season with garlic, chiles, cumin, and cilantro. Open kettle cooking time: 1½ to 2 hours. Pressure cooking time: soaked beans 25 minutes, unsoaked beans 30 minutes.

White (cannellini, Great Northern, navy): These oblong, cream-colored beans come in a variety of sizes. They have a mild flavor and slightly granular texture and are interchangeable in most recipes. Use white beans in soups, stews, casseroles, and baked beans. They combine well with celery, carrots, bell peppers, and tomatoes. Season with garlic, basil, rosemary, thyme, or oregano. Open kettle cooking time: 1½ hours. Pressure cooking time: soaked beans 25 minutes, unsoaked beans 30 minutes.

How to Cook Beans

Dry beans are notorious for containing small pebbles, field corn, etc. Pick through the beans well, and discard any foreign object or cracked or misshapen beans. Cover the beans with fresh, cold water, and soak overnight (or at least several hours). There are two reasons for soaking beans: it cuts down on the cooking time, and it removes some of the carbohydrates that cause flatulence (gas). After soaking, pour the water off (do not save it), and cover the beans again with fresh, cold water. Bring the beans to a full rolling boil, then reduce to a low boil, partially cover (to let the steam escape and prevent the pot from boiling over), and cook for 1 hour or longer until the beans are very tender. Now the beans are ready to use in your favorite recipe. Caution: Do not add salt or any ingredients containing salt to the beans until they are completely tender. Salt tends to enter the outer layer of the bean and seal it, not allowing water to enter the bean, so it may stay somewhat crunchy.

If this seems time-consuming, it's really not—it only takes a little work. Most of the time the beans are cooking. A pressure cooker will cut the cooking time by quite a bit. If you have a crock pot, it becomes very simple to

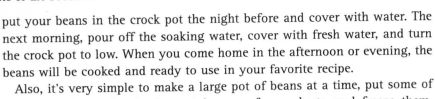

put your beans in the crock pot the night before and cover with water. The next morning, pour off the soaking water, cover with fresh water, and turn the crock pot to low. When you come home in the afternoon or evening, the beans will be cooked and ready to use in your favorite recipe.

Also, it's very simple to make a large pot of beans at a time, put some of the cooked beans in plastic containers or freezer bags, and freeze them. Beans freeze very well and it's simple to thaw them for a quick meal.

Grains

Rice

Rice is an essential part of Southwestern cuisine. Spanish rice, rice and beans in all of its many variations, rice pudding, and many other dishes make wonderful use of this grain. One of the easiest grains to digest, rice is a good choice for people with food allergies or sensitive digestive systems. Its protein is readily usable by the body. Unfortunately, most of the rice eaten in the world has been stripped of nutrients and flavor. But brown rice, with the bran and germ still intact, supplies more fiber, protein, B-vitamins, calcium, iron, and vitamin E than white rice. Brown rice comes in short-grain, medium-grain, and long-grain varieties. Short-grain and medium-grain brown rice have a tendency to be slightly sticky when cooked, which makes them an excellent choice for croquettes, rice puddings, cereals, or dishes where cooked rice is molded or shaped prior to serving. Long-grain brown rice is the most popular variety in America and is less sticky when cooked. The longer kernels separate when cooked and serve up light and fluffy. It works well in rice pilaf dishes, casseroles, salads, and Spanish rice or by itself as a side dish.

There are several varieties of rice that you may be unfamiliar with but are nonetheless delicious. Basmati rice has a nutty flavor and is available both as brown rice and naturally white rice. Although these aromatic, creamy, long-grain rices are native to the Himalayan foothills of Pakistan and India, basmati rice is also grown in California and Texas. The strain grown in Texas, white Texmati, is a cross between American long-grain rice and Asian basmati rice, with many of the nutritional advantages of brown rice and a flavor similar to basmati, though not quite as sweet.

Wehani rice is available from Lundberg Farms in California, where it was developed from seed originating in India. An interesting hybrid of tastes and textures, it has oversized grains which are amber in color, has a texture similar to wild rice, tastes like brown rice, and smells like popcorn when it is cooked!

How to Cook Rice

Here's a simple, fool-proof method for perfect brown rice every time. Begin by washing your rice well. I generally use a strainer and just rinse it with fresh, cold water. Place the rice in a pot with 2 parts water to each part rice. (Note: if you want creamy rice, as for cereal or rice pudding, use 3 parts water to 1 part rice.) Place the rice and water in a saucepan. Stir briefly, but do not stir again after that. Bring the water to a boil, then reduce to a low simmer. If you are using an electric stove, set it at the lowest setting. Cover with a tight fitting lid, and cook about 35 minutes. Do NOT stir your rice while it's cooking! Stirring will break the rice up and cause it to lump together. (Remember that long-grain rice will tend to stay separated and will fluff better than short-grain rice.)

After cooking for 35 minutes, remove the cover and gently tilt the pan to the side. If there is still water in the pot, cover and continue cooking until all the water is absorbed. Then remove the pot from the heat, cover, and let set about 5 minutes. Remove the lid and fluff with a fork. The rice is now ready to serve.

To store cooked rice, let it cool and place it in a plastic container with a tight fitting lid in the refrigerator.

Posole

A very close cousin to hominy, posole is kernels of corn that have been soaked with lime and then dried. As with beans, if posole is soaked for an hour or longer, the cooking time will be reduced: soaked posole will cook in about 40 minutes; unsoaked posole will take an hour or longer; pressure cooking posole will take about 15 to 20 minutes. Soaking also allows the kernels to swell to more than twice their original size. Posole cooks well with beans, and I often throw a handful of posole into my beans when putting them on to soak for chili or stews.

Chiles! (or Some Like It Hot!)

When the uninitiated "gringo" thinks of a south-of-the-border repast, there's generally one word that comes to mind—hot! While so many of us "fire-eaters" enjoy the hot chiles for which this cuisine is known, I most sincerely want to make it clear that hot chiles are only one part of the marvelous character of these dishes. In fact, because I know that the majority of guests I invite to my house for a "fiesta" do not like their food nearly as incendiary as I do, I tend to make my dishes quite mild and serve varying degrees of salsa or hot peppers on the side for the more adventurous. I've found it much easier to add heat to a dish than to try and take it away.

Chile peppers are probably one of the most misunderstood ingredients of Southwestern cuisine. The majority of those unfamiliar with chiles automatically think all varieties will cause smoke to puff from their ears after the first bite. Actually, there are a seemingly endless variety of chile peppers, and very many of them are in the sweet (no-fire-at-all) category. Among these are sweet red bell peppers, pimentos, squash peppers, and a few others. For those who like only a little "warmth" to their chiles, there are Anaheim peppers, poblanos, anchos (dried poblanos), New Mexican peppers, and pepperoncinis, among others. The hotter varieties include jalapeño, Santa Fe Grandes, Hungarian wax peppers, serranos, and cayenne. Then come the incendiary peppers (my favorites). These include Thai peppers, chiltepins, habaneros, and Scotch bonnets.

Fresh chiles should be roasted and peeled before using (the skins of peppers are bitter and not digestible); canned peppers have already been peeled before canning. There are several methods of roasting peppers depending on what type of stove or burner you use. Hold the chile with tongs or on a fork over the full flame of a gas burner, using a pot holder or oven mitt to protect your hand. Turn the pepper slowly until it becomes black and charred all over. With an electric stove, you can toast it under the broiler or in a heavy skillet until the skin chars and blackens. (I have a friend who uses a welder's torch to produce the same results. Not a common kitchen appliance, but it works.) To remove the skin, place the pepper in a bowl of cold water, and rub the peel a little; it will come right off.

Always handle the hotter peppers with care, and, whatever you do, don't rub your eyes! For some reason, whenever I cut hot peppers, my eye itches, and I rub it before I think! You may want to wear rubber gloves. Wash your hands well with soap after handling hot peppers to remove the oils that cause irritation.

Chiles are a wonderful source of vitamins (especially C and A). All chiles start out green and turn red as they ripen (or yellow, orange, or purple, depending on the variety). A red pepper, then, is not a separate variety of pepper from the green pepper, just ripe. Ripe peppers are also sweeter and easier to digest than green peppers.

Scientists have developed a chart measuring a unit of heat in peppers (called a Scoville unit) and ranking each pepper from 1 to 120, with 120 being the hottest. Red and green bell peppers rank at 1 with 0 S.U. The Anaheim ranks at about 3 with only 500-1,000 S.U. The jalapeño pepper that many find so excruciating only ranks about 15 with 4,000-5,000 S.U.! Serranos and chiltepins rate around 60 or so, while the habanero comes in at about 110 with 100,000-300,000 S.U.! What pepper ranks at 120? Rumor has it that there is a fireball in Thailand that is not yet commercially available. I, for one, anticipate its distribution with quivering taste buds.

Keep in mind that all of these rankings are approximate, and different peppers of the same variety will vary according to rainfall, amount of sun, etc. Sometimes even two peppers from the same plant will show remarkable differences. Also, be aware that the tip of a chile is milder than the upper part and that the membrane along the inside of the pepper is the hottest part.

Traditionally, many dishes blend two, three, or more chiles of complimentary flavors and degrees of hotness. As I said, I will generally use peppers with a rating of about a 5 or less in the main body of a dish and make a salsa or pepper chutney for the side, using a combination of chipotles, habaneros, and chiltepins combined with sautéed onion, garlic, and sun-dried tomatoes. I also place a warning sign (usually something humorous) by this spicy condiment so no one can accuse me of insensitivity to those less heat-tolerant.

Experiment with different varieties of fresh, canned, or dried peppers, enjoying the differences, both subtle and pronounced.

Southwest Spices and Herbs

Our Native American and Hispanic friends have been kind enough to share what they have learned about the fine art of seasoning. Cilantro is an important herb not only to Mexican and Southwestern cuisine, but also to Middle-Eastern and Asian dishes as well. This unique and flavorful herb is definitely best used when fresh and finely minced—dried cilantro is generally pretty flavorless. There are some people who don't care for the flavor of cilantro, in which case substitute either fresh oregano or Italian flat-leaf parsley. In some markets you may find it called Chinese parsley or fresh coriander—they're the same thing. Do not, however, substitute dried coriander. This is made from grinding the seed of the coriander plant and has a very different flavor. Cilantro is the leaf of the same plant. Try cilantro in bean dishes, as a salad green, with tomato dishes, with grains, or experiment with your own ideas.

Cumin seed or cumin seed powder is another unique flavor common to several ethnic cultures. Along with cilantro and chiles, cumin contributes to a large part of the personality of Mexican cooking. Not at all hot, cumin nonetheless adds passion to dishes.

Epazote has long been used in bean dishes in Mexico and has only recently been introduced in the Southwest. Besides imparting a delightful flavor and aroma, epazote can alleviate some of the flatulence (gas) problems often associated with eating beans. It may be more difficult to find than some more common herbs and spices, but is worth searching for.

New Flavors of the Southwest

Tofu

Tofu is easily one of the most versatile and popular foods in the world today, as it has been for over 2,000 years in China and Japan. And how, you might well ask, does an Asian staple like tofu fit into a book about Southwestern cuisine? Tofu's versatility has moved it well beyond the scope of being an "ethnic" ingredient. Because tofu can be made to resemble meat in many of its forms and because it so readily absorbs the flavors of whatever ingredients surround it, it adapts readily to any culture or cuisine.

You'll find two textures of tofu on the market: regular and silken. Regular tofu (or Japanese-style, as it is sometimes referred to) is very dense and chewy; silken tofu (Chinese-style) is custardy and silky, as its name would imply. Often both of these textures come in varying densities, usually soft, firm, and extra-firm. The soft tofu is used in salad dressings, dips, sauces, puddings, and smoothies. I often use soft tofu mixed in a blender with fresh fruit, a little ice, and, perhaps, a little raw honey or rice syrup to make a wonderful smoothie or shake. Firm tofu is often used in soups or salads, cut into cubes, or marinated for several hours in soy sauce, ginger, and garlic, then stir-fried with broccoli, shiitake mushrooms, and red bell peppers for a nice treat. Extra-firm tofu is perfect for stir-frying, marinated or not. I also like to broil ¼-inch thick slices of extra-firm tofu in a baking pan, browning a little on both sides, then topping with soy mozzarella and Parmesan and a marinara sauce. Bake the slices in a 350°F oven for 35 to 40 minutes. This makes a great tofu Parmesan. To make your tofu even firmer, try pressing it. Line a bread pan with a few layers of paper towel or a clean dish towel, place your tofu on that, add more toweling, and then another bread pan. Place a heavy jar or cans on top, and let it set for 2 to 3 hours. That will press much of the water out and make the tofu much firmer.

Another means of making the tofu firm and chewy is to freeze it, then defrost, drain, and press it. The texture will be quite similar to chicken chunks; if crumbled, it will resemble ground beef. Season it with a little soy sauce, poultry seasoning, chili powder, or whatever flavoring you like. Cook

it with some onions, garlic, tomatoes, and chiles, and use in place of ground beef on tacos or in enchiladas.

Steaming tofu will generally give it a nice chewy texture as well. Try steaming ½-inch thick slices of tofu for about 20 to 30 minutes, marinate it with your favorite vinaigrette dressing for a couple of hours, then grill or broil. Top with a shiitake mushroom sauce. Delicious!

Because tofu is perishable, it should be stored in the refrigerator covered with fresh water. Change the water at least every other day. If the tofu turns yellow and develops an off odor, it has gotten spoiled. Sometimes if you catch it before it gets that far, you can soak it in a little lemon water, and that will refresh it.

Several of the recipes in this book incorporate tofu, or tofu may be nicely substituted for another ingredient with very tasty and nutritious results. Feel free to experiment with tofu in all of your cooking adventures!

Tempeh

Tempeh is made from either soybeans or a combination of grains or grains and beans. A cultured mushroom fiber is grown on the beans, which binds them together into a solid cake. Tempeh has been a common food in the Far East for hundreds of years. Being a cultured product, tempeh is very easily digested, and the nutrients it contains are easily assimilated by the body. Like tofu, tempeh is cholesterol-free and low in saturated fat and calories.

Because tempeh has a chewier texture than tofu, many people take readily to its use as a replacement for meat in many dishes. It's generally found in the frozen food section of your natural foods store.

Textured vegetable protein

Textured vegetable protein is processed from soy flour to resemble ground meat or meat chunks. Because it's a dry product you rehydrate before using, it's great to keep on hand for "last minute" meal ideas. Like tofu, textured vegetable protein will take on the flavors of the foods it's cooked with. Flavored product is also available, but is usually higher in sodium than unflavored varieties.

Seitan

Seitan is made from the protein, or gluten, of wheat flour. It has been used for centuries in Japan and the Far East to make foods that taste and look like meat. Seitan is also cholesterol-free, very low in fat and calories, and a great source of protein. It can be purchased fresh or frozen, or it can be made from wheat flour, water, and seasonings. You can also find mixes at your natural foods market.

Sun-Dried Tomatoes

Tomatoes play an important role in Southwestern cuisine, and sun-dried tomatoes are adding a new dimension. Like other fruits, tomatoes become quite concentrated in nutrients, calories, and flavor when they are dried. If stored in a bag or jar in a dark, dry place, they will keep for long periods of time. Sun-dried tomatoes become very sweet and flavorful when soaked in water, oil, or other liquids until they soften. Chop into little pieces and add to soups, stews, pasta sauces, casseroles, pizzas, or other dishes. Use your imagination and experiment with them on sandwiches and salads.

Sometimes you can find sun-dried tomatoes already hydrated and packed in olive oil. While very tasty, go lightly with these as they will add a lot of fat to whatever they're added to. Sun-dried tomatoes hydrate just as well in water or wine and contain less fat that way.

Artichokes

Artichokes grow very well in home gardens throughout the Southwest and are an excellent accompaniment or beginning to a meal. I have several artichoke plants in my garden, and in season I can cut a couple of large bulbs and steam them when friends gather for an evening of music and conversation. An artichoke is actually the flowering bulb of the plant before blossoming. They are available most of the year in the supermarket. (The harvest time in home gardens will vary as to geographic location.) Look for fresh, firm bulbs with, perhaps, a hint of purple or black.

The quickest and simplest way to prepare artichokes is to steam them. Simply cut off the top third of the bulb (a serrated knife works best) and the top third of each leaf (use heavy scissors). Scoop out the middle of the bulb (including the fuzzy bottom), but be sure to leave the heart; it's the best part. Place the artichoke upside down in a hot steamer basket; you might want to pull the leaves apart a little first so the steam will penetrate the whole bulb. Steam about 20 minutes, or until a butter knife inserts easily into the bottom of the bulb. Serve with lemon juice or dill sauce, and enjoy!

Artichokes are generally eaten by pulling the leaves out individually, dipping in juice or sauce, and scraping the fleshy part of the leaf along your top front teeth to remove it. After the leaves are all eaten comes the real treat—the heart of the artichoke. Cut away the hairy filaments and any of the stem, and savor what is left. Yum!

Sweeteners

Many people are rethinking their use of sweeteners, whether it's because they're watching their weight or because too many sweets can compromise their health. Although white sugar in moderation probably does little immediate damage to the body, there are sweeteners with higher nutritional value and, certainly, much more flavor. Also of interest to vegans is that much white sugar is filtered through bone char, the charred animal bones that are a by-product from slaughter houses. There is no way of telling when you buy white sugar if bone char or granular carbon filtering was used in the processing. The bottom line with white sugar is that it is a poor quality source of nutrients and flavor, easily eclipsed by other, higher quality products. Consider some of the following sweeteners.

Granulated Sweeteners

Date Sugar: Date sugar is simply dried, ground dates and contains most of the nutrition of the original fruit. It does not dissolve well but has a wonderful flavor and is good in baking.

Sucanat: Sucanat is made from evaporated, granulated sugar cane juice and retains all of the complex sugar, vitamins, minerals, and enzymes (including the one that prevents tooth decay). It has much more flavor than white or brown sugar and makes an excellent substitute for either. Keep in mind, however, that Sucanat will affect the blood sugar level in the same way as white sugar, so it should be used in moderation. Diabetics should avoid it altogether.

Liquid Sweeteners

Amasake: Amasake is a whole-grain sweetener made by adding cultured brown rice to cooked rice. It has a thick, pudding-like consistency and is sweet but also easy to digest. Amasake may be diluted with water and used as a milk substitute in many recipes. Although it may be a little trickier to use than more familiar sweeteners, I recommend experimenting with it as a more nutritious alternative to other sweeteners.

Blackstrap molasses: Blackstrap is the liquid that is left from processing white sugar after all the sucrose crystals have been removed. It is a VERY strongly flavored sweetener, and only a small amount is needed in most recipes. Blackstrap and Sucanat are the only processed sweeteners that have a high nutrient content. Blackstrap is rich in minerals, especially iron and calcium. Buy only unsulfured molasses (see page 22).

Brown rice syrup or barley malt syrup: Both syrups are made by using malt enzymes to convert the starch in rice or barley to sugar. They are broken down much more slowly in the body than most other sugars, including fructose, thus they may sometimes be tolerated in small amounts (with a nutritional counselor's approval) by people with diabetes or hypoglycemia. Brown rice syrup and barley malt syrup are excellent substitutes for corn sweetener, and because they are more flavorful, less is needed in recipes.

Fresh or dried fruit or fruit juice concentrate: Probably the most nutritious way to add sweetness to your foods is by using fresh or dried fruit. They are whole foods that have had little or no processing and contain vitamins, minerals, and fiber. Try chopping, dicing, or even blending fresh fruits like bananas, pears, etc., to use in place of other sweeteners in your recipes. Or soak a few raisins, figs, or currants, and add to your recipes either chopped or whole. Instead of sugar on your cereal, try sliced bananas, berries, or raisins.

Fruit juice concentrate is usually purchased frozen, and water is added to make juice. However, undiluted, thawed concentrate can be a tasty substitute for other sugars. Try a little apple juice concentrate in your oatmeal, for instance. Frozen concentrate is also a tasty addition to smoothies. Thawed concentrate will keep up to a month in your refrigerator. Because dried fruits and juice concentrates often contain dangerous levels of pesticides, organic brands are suggested.

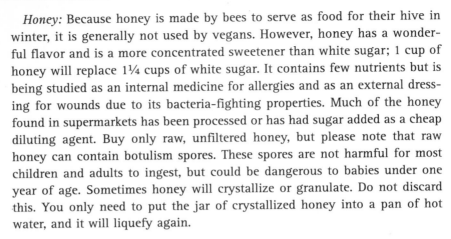

Honey: Because honey is made by bees to serve as food for their hive in winter, it is generally not used by vegans. However, honey has a wonderful flavor and is a more concentrated sweetener than white sugar; 1 cup of honey will replace 1¼ cups of white sugar. It contains few nutrients but is being studied as an internal medicine for allergies and as an external dressing for wounds due to its bacteria-fighting properties. Much of the honey found in supermarkets has been processed or has had sugar added as a cheap diluting agent. Buy only raw, unfiltered honey, but please note that raw honey can contain botulism spores. These spores are not harmful for most children and adults to ingest, but could be dangerous to babies under one year of age. Sometimes honey will crystallize or granulate. Do not discard this. You only need to put the jar of crystallized honey into a pan of hot water, and it will liquefy again.

Maple syrup: Maple syrup is a delicious sweetener, but it sometimes contains animal fats (such as lard or butter) added to the processing to reduce foaming. Grade B maple syrup actually has more flavor than grade A and is especially preferable for baking. Always use real maple syrup on your pancakes and waffles instead of maple-flavored syrup, which is usually corn syrup and sugar with a little maple flavoring added.

Molasses: Molasses is sugar cane juice from which the white sugar has been extracted. Its flavor is quite strong and much less is needed in recipes than most other sweeteners. It has a small amount of nutrients, including calcium and iron, but otherwise has been as highly processed as white sugar. Use in moderation. Avoid sulfured molasses. (Unless marked unsulfured, it probably contains sulfur.) Sulfur, a preservative, adds an unpleasant flavor and may be a health hazard for many people, especially asthmatics.

Sorghum molasses: Sorghum molasses is made by crushing the stalks of sorghum (a cereal grain) and boiling the juice to make syrup. It is very tasty on pancakes and waffles.

Carob

Carob is generally known as a chocolate substitute (although I prefer to think of chocolate as a carob substitute). It has a richer, earthier flavor than chocolate. Carob is made by grinding the bean pods of a variety of locust tree. When the Bible refers to Jesus or St. John as living on a diet of locusts and honey, it refers to carob, not sweetened insects. Carob was a common food of that historical period, and a type of bread made from carob flour and honey was often eaten while travelling or during retreats.

Carob is very nutritious, with a fairly high content of vitamins and minerals. It is lower in fat than chocolate and is naturally sweeter, thus needing less added sweetener.

Chocolate, is lower in nutrients, and contains caffeine and theobromine, both having an effect on the body similar to a low dose of amphetimines. Studies done on children having 3 chocolate bars and 3 caffeinated sodas daily have equated these dosages, due to the children's smaller body size, with the high experienced by some "speed" addicts. Thus, when people crave chocolate, it is often the feeling of these drugs they crave.

Chocolate (as well as spinach and a few other foods) is also high in oxalic acid, one of the more common food allergens (a substance that triggers an allergic reaction). This can manifest itself in the body in many ways, but one of the most common symptoms is a migraine headache. Someone could experience frequent migraines and be searching for a stronger pain killer while, at the same time, munching on a chocolate bar.

Carob powder can be purchased either raw or roasted and will substitute in recipes for equal amounts of cocoa powder. Raw carob has a few more nutrients, but many prefer the flavor of roasted carob powder.

Carob candy bars in health food stores are sometimes not as nutritious as would be expected. They are usually an improvement over commercial chocolate, but they often contain hydrogenated tropical oils or saturated fats, processed sugars, and other additives. It's best either to eat these sparingly or make your own carob candies at home for a nutritious, delicious alternative. Experiment!

Egg Substitutes

So, you've decided to give up eggs. Scrambled tofu makes a great breakfast, but how do you go about substituting eggs in your favorite recipes? In many recipes, such as pancakes, you can just omit the eggs altogether. Try some of the following different egg alternatives, and see what you like best:

Ener-G Egg Replacer - A popular egg substitute made from potato starch, tapioca flour, leavening agents (calcium lactate [vegan], calcium carbonate, and citric acid), and a gum derived from cottonseed. It's primarily intended to replace the leavening/binding characteristics of eggs in baking, but it can also be used for nonbaked foods and quiches.

(These are especially helpful as binding agents):
• One-quarter cup blended soft tofu can be substituted for 1 egg. Or try the same quantity of mashed beans, mashed potatoes, or nut butters.
• Add one tablespoon ground flax seeds (use an electric coffee mill or blender to grind) to 3 tablespoons boiling water, and let steep for about 10 minutes or until it becomes gelatinous.

(These are good for adding moisture when replacing eggs):
• ½ mashed banana, ¼ cup applesauce or puréed fruit, or 1 teaspoon soy flour mixed with 1 tablespoon water
• If you don't mind using eggs but want to cut back on fat and cholesterol, use 2 egg whites to replace one whole egg. (There are only 15 calories and no fat or cholesterol in each egg white.)

More Food Tips

Baking powder: Avoid brands that have aluminum.

Buttermilk: Most commercial buttermilk is now low fat and is an excellent ingredient in baking. It helps provide leavening when using baking soda.

Flours: Buy only whole-grain flours, and store them in the refrigerator or freezer to prevent rancidity and vitamin loss.

Lecithin: An oil that occurs naturally in soybeans and can be mixed in a 1 to 1 ratio with canola oil to coat pots and pans and give them a non-stick finish.

Margarine: If you wish to use margarine, try Spectrum Spread. It is the only non-hydrogenated margarine, as well as being free of dairy, chemicals, and low in saturates.

Nuts: Buy fresh, raw, unsalted nuts, and store them in the refrigerator or freezer to preserve nutrients and prevent rancidity.

Oils: Buy only cold-pressed oils or extra-virgin olive oil, and store them in the refrigerator. (Olive oil will get a bit cloudy when cold, so you may want to let it set at room temperature for just a few minutes before using.) Either canola or flaxseed get high ratings for their nutrient content, but olive oil is also a good choice. So-called "light" oils may be lighter in flavor, but have just as many calories as their regular counterparts. Avoid all oils that are solid or thick at room temperature or otherwise high in saturated fats (coconut or palm oil and, to a lesser extent, cottonseed oil). Do not cook with safflower oil.

Strongly flavored oils may be used in small quantities to impart their special flavor (toasted sesame oil, hazelnut oil, almond oil, etc.). Peanut oil is sometimes used for cooking at high temperatures because it has a very high burning temperature. If any oil develops an "off" odor or flavor, discard it.

Sprouts: When growing your own sprouts, use only seeds that have not been fumigated or treated with fungicides or pesticides, as have most seeds from nurseries or seed markets. Buy seeds meant for human consumption from the health food store.

Vanilla: Use only the vanilla bean or a pure extract.

Yogurt: Look for yogurt that has a live, viable, or active culture. Those words should be right on the yogurt container; if not, don't buy it. Better yet, make your own yogurt. Soy yogurt is also available.

Putting in a Good Word for Organic Foods

Foods are labeled "organic" if they are produced by farming methods that maintain and replenish the fertility of the soil, using compost and natural fertilizers such as animal manure. Organic crops are produced without the use of synthetic pesticides and fertilizers. Organic foods are minimally processed to maintain the integrity of the food without artificial ingredients, preservatives, or irradiation. Before the intensive use of chemical fertilizers, pesticides, and herbicides that began after World War II, most farm crops were produced using organic farming methods, although it wasn't called "organic" at the time.

Many of the pesticides that are now being linked to cancer and other diseases were approved by government agencies before research showed how dangerous they are. A report by the National Academy of Sciences estimates that pesticides might be responsible for as many as 4 million cancer cases among Americans. It's important to remember, also, that children are four times more likely to be harmed by pesticides and other toxic residues than adults. Farm workers and harvesters are at increased risk from these chemicals as well. Not only have these chemicals been shown to cause cancer, but they are linked to birth defects, genetic mutations, and nerve damage as well.

Commercial farming methods are basically at odds with nature and the environment. Organic farming methods, on the other hand, are in harmony with nature, creating and supporting a healthy, balanced bio-system. Where commercial farming methods see wildlife and insects as harmful to the system, organic farmers incorporate them into the system, using beneficial insects to help control the balance, much as nature does. Fence rows, wetlands, and other natural areas improve the health of the organic farm by encouraging a better balance of wildlife beneficial to the crops. For example, providing shelter for foxes, birds, and other small animals helps control rodents and other crop-damaging animals and insects.

While commercial farming methods tend to deplete the soil of nutrients, organic farmers build healthy soil through mulching and composting, crop rotation, and just allowing nature to take her course. This greatly enhances the fertility of the soil for future crops.

Besides providing more nutritious food for the individual, organic farming makes for a healthier rural community by supporting small family farms. The small organic farmer is more apt to preserve the bio-diversity of the food supply, taking the initiative to increase the types and varieties of crops grown and initiating research into farming methods that are based on health and environment rather than profitability.

Another common misconception about organic foods is that they are more expensive than non-organic foods. Even though organic foods might have a higher "shelf cost" than commercial produce, there are hidden costs involved with commercial produce that may not show up in the cost of a head of lettuce. In the long run, the consumer does pay an indirect cost for cleanup of polluted water, the replacement of badly eroded soils, pesticide regulation and testing, the disposal and cleanup of hazardous wastes, and the costs of health care for farmers and their workers. As an example, a recent study at Cornell University disclosed some of the annual environmental costs for conventional farming methods:

Damage to agricultural ecosystems- $525 million

Pesticide poisonings and related illnesses- $250 million

Pesticide regulation and monitoring- $150 million

Testing drinking water for pesticide contamination- $1.3 billion

Also, studies have shown organically grown foods to be higher in many nutrients, as well as being free of health-damaging pesticides, herbicides, and chemical preservatives. Spending a few extra pennies on organically grown produce will save dollars on doctors and other health care bills.

And if health concerns, environmental challenges, and economic value are not reason enough to buy "organic," let the wholesome, nourishing taste of fruits and vegetables grown without toxic residues and poisons convince you. Organic foods taste better and are more satisfying than their commercial counterparts. Many chefs and home cooks are now buying organic foods because they taste better and help us to feel better. Why would anyone who cares about their health and their families, the health of the planet, and health of the economic community ever choose anything but 100 percent organic?

THE ART OF COOKING: KITCHEN EQUIPMENT

It's certainly not necessary to go out and buy a lot of fancy equipment or have your kitchen redone in order to enjoy tasty, nutritious meals. I recently met a young couple who had been living in a tent for several months while building their home. They made marvelous gourmet meals on a camping stove.

The main goal in setting up your kitchen is to make it comfortable for you. Love your kitchen, make it a place where you celebrate cooking, honoring the spirits of nurturing, your expression of love for yourself, your family, and your friends, where you may feel relaxed and at ease yet somewhat excited at the miracles you are about to perform.

Place your tools and utensils where they will be convenient to the job at hand but will not interfere or become a nuisance. Hooks on the wall and shelves and drawers should be situated so as to simplify and facilitate ease of movement. Do not clutter the work area with utensils and gadgets that look cute but are never used. Simplify!

A few practical tools and utensils will go far in making cooking an enjoyable experience, especially when you learn to use them well. Here are some I consider essential.

The Stove

It's possible to cook over just about any source of heat–gas, electric, microwave, candles, sterno, campfire, fireplace, solar, or even over a hot automobile engine. I think most people will agree that the means of cooking has a greater effect on the finished dish than just "how many degrees at what length of time?" For years I have preferred gas stoves to electric, although I could never quite put my finger on the complete reason. Perhaps it's just me, but I feel that it's easier and more enjoyable to cook with gas than electric (you get an immediate response to the controls, for one thing), and, because of that, the experience of cooking and eating are enhanced. Talking to other chefs, cooks, and nutritionists through the years, I have found many with similar opinions.

Microwave cooking, though in vogue and touted by many "scientific" nutritionists, is best simply ignored and avoided. It alters the foods in undesirable ways, as many foods come out unpalatable and rubbery (baked potatoes, for instance). It does the job but is the quality of the food what you want it to be? It's really not that difficult or time-consuming to cook from scratch with a few time-saving tips and techniques.

Knives and Cleavers

Other than the stove, the most important tools in the kitchen are the knives. A good set of several select knives are to a cook as the brushes are to a painter. And the way the cook uses his knives, his artistic technique, are as the brush stokes of the artist.

It's not necessary to have many knives, just the right ones. Most cooks are very comfortable with a good chef's knife (sometimes called a French knife), a serrated knife, a paring knife, and perhaps a cleaver. If you're a vegetarian, you won't need carving knives or boning knives, obviously.

The chef's knife is one of the handiest tools in the kitchen, yet it's the one many cooks either don't have or avoid using. This is the big one, (usually an 8-inch to 12-inch blade), often with a long curved edge to the blade. Even though it might appear menacing to some, it is the most practical and useful knife for most chopping, dicing, and slicing. Because it is the best tool for the job, it's also the safest.

To demonstrate that point, I've seen many experienced cooks trying to slice carrots with a paring knife. It's a very inefficient use of energy. The paring knife was designed for a different job–small, detailed garnishing and intricate work. You have to work far too hard to chop large vegetables with your paring knife. You begin to believe you don't like to cook–it's too much work. You become frustrated and careless, and that's when an accident is likely to happen.

The chef's knife, on the other hand, was designed specifically for chopping. The long bevelled (curved) edge gives the knife a rocking motion that has more leverage and weight behind it, making chopping almost effortless. The back edge of the knife, the two to three inches closest to the handle, should have the sharpest edge, and this is the part of the knife you want to cut the food with. Place that part of the knife above the food you want to cut, and place the tip of the knife on the cutting board so that the knife is at about a 30 to 40 degree angle to your body. Hold the food to be cut firmly, with your hand well back and the fingers curved down, out of the way of the knife. Without lifting the tip from the cutting board, push down with the handle of

the knife toward the cutting board, giving the knife just a little slide forward as you come down. Leaving the tip of the knife still on the cutting board, lift the handle until the blade just clears the top of the vegetable. Keeping the knife in place, slide the vegetable over for the next cut.

A serrated knife with a jagged or uneven cutting edge, is generally used for slicing softer foods (ripe tomatoes, bread, etc.) that would tend to be mashed by the weight of the chef's knife. Use it with a sawing, back-and-forth motion.

A small paring knife should have a sharp point and edge and is used for jobs where a large knife would be unwieldy. Use it for making garnishes, coring tomatoes (don't hold the tomato in your hand; it's dangerous), peeling potatoes (you have to hold the potato, but be careful), and so on.

Used in much the same way as the chef's knife, the cleaver is a useful tool for chopping, having considerable weight behind it. Buy one with a bevelled edge to get that rocking motion as you would with a chef's knife.

Almost as important as the knives, is a good sharpening tool of some sort. A sharpening rod, either of steel or stone, or even the little gadget on the back of an electric can opener will provide a good temporary edge and should be used every time you use your knife. Unless you have the right tools and experience, I recommend taking your knives to a professional to have them sharpened once or twice a year to give them a more permanent edge. Do not be intimidated by a sharp knife; it's much safer than a dull one, which will bounce off of whatever you're trying to cut. Generally, that's when accidents happen.

Other Helpful Kitchen Tools

It's also important to own a good cutting board. Fortunately, it needn't be expensive. An excellent wooden cutting board can be made from a piece of oak or other hard, non-splintering wood, 2 feet square and 2 inches thick. The edges should be well-sanded, and there should be no loose splinters or cracks in which bacteria may harbor. Do not treat the cutting board with any sealer, stain, or other chemical that you would not want in your food. You can also buy good wooden or plastic cutting boards. Do not use wood for any type of meat or fish as the juices will seep into the wood and the bacteria will contaminate anything else cut on the board. If you do not cook meat, poultry, or fish, it's not as much of a problem, but always clean your cutting board well. Even fruits and vegetables can be contaminated. Whatever you choose, make sure it is large enough. I've witnessed cooks struggling with a tiny cutting board (usually cut into some cute, but impractical, shape) that's hardly big enough to hold a good-sized carrot.

Also helpful are:

- measuring spoons and cups (if you need exact measurements)
- scissors
- wire whisk
- 4-sided grater
- large colander
- soup ladle
- slotted spoon
- set of glass or ceramic mixing bowls
- stiff vegetable brush
- assortment of wooden spoons

Although I seldom need one, I keep a small, hand-held can-opener. It's less expensive, works as well, and won't break down as easily as an expensive electric one.

Cookware

There are companies that make a fortune selling expensive and fancy cookware that will become obsolete in a few years or become damaged and useless. Avoid the use of aluminum and nonstick cookware. Aluminum cookware is suspected of having a link to Alzheimer's disease. The surface of nonstick cookware will eventually become scratched and worn. Some of the particles from the surface will eventually migrate into the food you cook.

Actually I've used the same cast-iron and stainless steel cookware for more than 25 years or so, and it doesn't seem to get any worse as the years go by. I generally have three cast-iron skillets of various sizes and a large cast-iron Dutch oven stacked on my stove at all times ready to cook with. Some of these skillets are 30 years old now, and I honestly don't know how I would be able to do without them. Cast-iron cookware heats well and evenly, is simple to care for, does not become a health hazard like aluminum or nonstick surfaces, and actually adds iron to your diet whenever you eat food cooked in it.

When you buy a brand new cast-iron skillet, it won't have that seasoned black patina that comes with use. You will need to season it before you use

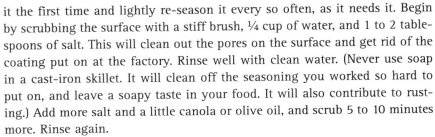

it the first time and lightly re-season it every so often, as it needs it. Begin by scrubbing the surface with a stiff brush, ¼ cup of water, and 1 to 2 table-spoons of salt. This will clean out the pores on the surface and get rid of the coating put on at the factory. Rinse well with clean water. (Never use soap in a cast-iron skillet. It will clean off the seasoning you worked so hard to put on, and leave a soapy taste in your food. It will also contribute to rust-ing.) Add more salt and a little canola or olive oil, and scrub 5 to 10 minutes more. Rinse again.

If possible, depending on how much time and energy you want to put into it, rub the cooking surface well with more oil. If your skillet does not have a wooden handle, place it in a preheated 400°F oven, and bake for about 15 minutes. Carefully remove it (it will be very hot), and add more oil. Place it back into the oven again for another 15 minutes or so. Remove and oil again. If this seems like a lot of work, don't panic. Do as much as you can. The more you use your skillet, the better the seasoning will become. Just be careful not to remove the oil you've already worked into the surface by washing it with soap. If it gets too dry or food begins to stick, rub a little more oil into the surface.

To clean your skillet after using, rinse with hot water and scrub with the type of plastic scrubbie usually suggested for cleaning Teflon. If food is cooked or dried on, bring an inch or so of water to a boil in the pan. The food should loosen up and come right off. Re-oil, if needed. With care, your cast-iron cookware will last for generations.

Other cookware you will find useful is:

- a stainless steel muffin pan
- 2 to 3 baking sheets
- several pie pans and bread pans
- a set of ovenproof Pyrex or glass casserole dishes

You might consider a few optional tools for convenience sake, but I've been able to get along without them pretty well when they weren't available. An electric blender, food processor, or electric mixer will make some jobs a little easier or make the end result a little nicer. Also nice to have is a pres-sure cooker. It can really cut down on the cooking time, especially with beans. Or, if time is not a problem but timing is, consider a crock-pot or slow-cooker. They're great for beans or soups.

This, then, is my idea of a well-equipped kitchen. Of course, if you find that gadgets and specialized tools make the job easier or more enjoyable for you, be my guest. When you enjoy what you do, it shows in the results, and, as the old saying goes, "the proof of the pudding is in the tasting."

Glossary of Unusual Ingredients

Agar: A vegetable gelatin made from sea algae. Available at Oriental markets or health food stores.

Balsamic vinegar: A rich-tasting, aromatic wine vinegar aged in wooden vats to produce a unique flavor. Balsamic vinegar brings out the flavor of many foods, even fruits. Try adding ½ teaspoon balsamic vinegar and ½ teaspoon vanilla extract to a fresh fruit salad, then refrigerate an hour or longer. The fruit will be juicier and sweeter!

Bran: Use unprocessed or miller's bran, not bran cereal which is generally high in sugar and other additives. Bran is a wonderful source of fiber.

Flax seeds: An oily seed with a slightly laxative effect that is also a good source of omega-3 fatty acids (shown to help break up cholesterol in the bloodstream). Can be mixed with hot water in a blender to make a substitute for eggs.

Miso: Miso is a concentrated soybean paste with a flavor like thick, strong soy sauce. It is rich in protein, B-vitamins, minerals, and digestive enzymes, and is also very salty, so omit salt or other salty foods or condiments when using it. Miso is often used to give a bouillon flavor and added nutrition to soups, stews, and sauces. Add it at the end of cooking and do not boil, so that the enzymes it contains are not destroyed.

Peanut butter (and other nut butters): Buy brands made with nuts only—no sugars, salt, emulsifiers, or stabilizers. If the oil separates out, just stir it back in, or pour it off and use it for cooking. If your peanut butter becomes a bit

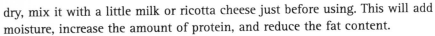

dry, mix it with a little milk or ricotta cheese just before using. This will add moisture, increase the amount of protein, and reduce the fat content.

Tamari: In the Orient, tamari is a wheat-free soy sauce, as opposed to a product called shoyu, which contains wheat. In the U.S. all three terms are used somewhat interchangeably. Buy only natural, aged soy sauce (instead of chemically fermented); the best source is the health food store.

Umeboshi plum paste: A salty purée of Japanese plums, used for its health-giving qualities as well as its flavor.

Wheat germ: Wheat germ is high in protein, B-complex vitamins, vitamin E, potassium, and zinc. These nutrients will last longer if the wheat germ is stored in the refrigerator or freezer.

Whole wheat pastry flour: Pastry flour is made from soft spring wheat, as opposed to bread flour, which is made from hard winter wheat. It contains little or no gluten, the substance that gives bread its stretchy quality, so it is generally not desirable for yeast breads unless mixed with whole wheat or gluten flour. As with other flours, store in the refrigerator or freezer.

SPANISH TERMS
FOR METHODS OR INGREDIENTS

Ajo - garlic

Al horno - oven-baked

Ancho - a poblano chile that has been dried

Antojito - appetizer or hors d'oeuvre

Arroz - rice

Asar - to roast or broil

Barbacoa - barbecue

Borracho - cooked with wine; literally, "drunk"

Bunuelo - pastry that is deep fried until it becomes puffy

Burro (burrito) - large flour tortilla wrapped around a filling

Calabaza - pumpkin or squash

Caldo - soup or broth

Caliente - hot (temperature)

Canela - cinnamon

Cazuela - stew pot

Cebolla - onion

Cerveza - beer

Chilaquiles - corn tortilla pieces covered with enchilada sauce and cheese, then baked in a casserole

Chili powder - usually a blend of dried ground chiles and other seasonings, such as oregano, cumin, garlic, and onion powder

Chiltepins or Chilepequins - a variety of chiles

Chimichanga - a deep-fried burro—literally, "thingamajig"

Cilantro - the leaf of the coriander plant, also called Chinese parsley

Coco - coconut

Comal - heavy, round griddle for baking tortillas

Cumino - cumin seeds, ground or whole, used to season and flavor

Ejote - string bean

Empenada - a turnover

Enchilada - a corn tortilla dipped in red chile sauce, filled with vegetables, cheese, nuts, or just about anything else, topped with sauce and cheese, and baked

Enrollado - rolled

Ensalada - salad

Escabeche - pickled

Fideos - thin pasta

Flan - a baked custard with caramel sauce

Flauta - filled corn tortilla that has been deep fried; literally, "flute"

Frijoles - beans

Garbanzo - chick-peas

Gazpacho - a cold, spicy tomato-based soup

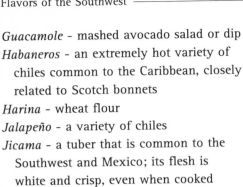

Guacamole - mashed avocado salad or dip

Habaneros - an extremely hot variety of chiles common to the Caribbean, closely related to Scotch bonnets

Harina - wheat flour

Jalapeño - a variety of chiles

Jicama - a tuber that is common to the Southwest and Mexico; its flesh is white and crisp, even when cooked

Lechuga - lettuce

Maiz - corn

Mano - a piece of volcanic rock used for grinding ingredients; literally, "hand"

Mantequilla - butter

Masa - dough, usually corn or hominy

Menudo - soup commonly made with tripe; it can be made vegetarian

Miel - honey

Mole - sauce made from chiles and unsweetened chocolate (carob may be used instead)

Naranja - orange

Nixtamal - hominy (also called posole)

Nopales - cooked cactus pads

Pan - bread

Pepino - cucumber

Pepitos - pumpkin seeds

Picante - hot (to the taste), spicy

Pimienta - black pepper

Poblano - a variety of chile

Postre - dessert

Quesadilla - Mexican grilled cheese, made with a tortilla instead of bread

Queso - cheese

Rabano - radish

Relleno - stuffed

Repollo - cabbage

Ristra - a string of dried, red chiles

Sal - salt

Salsa - sauce

Sangria - a drink made from fruit juices and wine

Sopa - soup

Taco - a corn tortilla folded over a filling

Tamales - a corn husk, stuffed with masa, beans, cheese, or chiles, then steamed

Topopo - a salad shaped like a volcano

Tortilla - a thin, unleavened bread made with wheat flour or corn masa

Tostada - toasted, as toasted tortillas

BREAKFAST

Pancake Tips

There are a few basic rules for pancakes that seem to help them turn out better.

1) Heat the skillet or griddle before baking the pancakes. I prefer a heavy cast-iron skillet, well seasoned. Use a low to medium flame (a little lower for sourdough pancakes). If you're using an electric griddle, use the 350°F temperature setting. A good way to tell if the cooking surface is hot enough is to sprinkle a few drops of water on it. If they seem to dance around on the surface for 2 to 3 seconds, it's ready. If they do nothing, the griddle is not hot enough. If they evaporate immediately, it's too hot.

2) Mix all of your dry ingredients in one bowl, and combine well before adding wet ingredients. Do NOT beat your pancake batter. Gently mix or fold it only until all the dry ingredients are moistened. If it still has a few small lumps, that's alright. Let your pancake batter stand for about 5 to 10 minutes before using. This improves the texture.

3) Very important—pancakes are not fried, they are baked! Do NOT put oil onto your griddle. If your griddle is clean and well-seasoned, the oil in the batter will be enough to keep them from sticking. If they stick, you are trying to turn them too soon (see next tip).

4) Bake the first side until the bubbles in the middle of the pancake burst and the surface loses its gloss. Bake the second side about 2 minutes. (Sourdough pancakes usually take a little longer to bake at a slightly lower temperature.) When you think they are ready to turn, gently lift one side with the spatula. It should be golden brown. If not, or if they tend to stick, wait a few moments longer.

5) Turn your pancakes gently; flipping them up in the air may look spectacular but makes flat pancakes. Also, resist the urge to flatten them with the spatula. You want light, fluffy pancakes.

I would like to suggest avoiding the use of white flour, either bleached or unbleached. I prefer, instead, to use whole wheat pastry flour. It contains the germ and bran (and flavor) of a good whole wheat flour but is softer and finer and makes nice, light pancakes. Experiment with spelt, teff, barley, or other flours, or use a blend of two or three flours. Half whole wheat pastry flour and half buckwheat flour makes a wonderfully hearty buckwheat pancake. Because sourdough requires yeast, you might want to add 2 teaspoons vital wheat gluten to your batter or dough per cup of flour if you're using a lower gluten flour like pastry flour. If you feel the need to have lighter pancakes, substitute a little unbleached, unenriched white flour for part of the whole grain flour, but try to use as little as possible.

Caramelized Mango-Orange Pancakes

Yield: 4 servings

These rich, sweet pancakes make an elegant dessert as well as a terrific breakfast. Try them topped with a low-fat nondairy frozen dessert!

Mix the pancake ingredients gently but thoroughly into a smooth batter, and set aside.

To make the filling, grate the rind from the oranges, and set it aside. Peel and segment the oranges. In a heavy skillet, melt the butter, and add the sweetener. Add the mangoes and oranges (including the rind), and cook 4 to 5 minutes over medium heat to caramelize the fruit. Add the Grand Marnier, if desired, and the pistachios. Cook another 3 to 4 minutes. Cover and keep warm.

Heat a heavy skillet or crêpe pan over medium heat, pour in a little of the pancake batter, and gently swirl in the pan to make a thin pancake. Cook for about 2 minutes, or until browned. Gently turn and cook on the other side. Repeat with remaining mixture. Serve with the caramelized fruit, and garnish with a fresh mint sprig. Enjoy!

VARIATIONS

Substitute apples, pears, papaya, or other fruit.

Pancake batter:
1¼ cups whole wheat pastry flour
1 tablespoon sweetener
Egg replacer equivalent to 3 eggs, p. 24, or 2 ripe bananas, mashed
1 teaspoon aluminum-free baking powder
1 tablespoon cold-pressed canola oil
Enough soymilk or rice milk to make a medium-thin batter

Filling:
1 tablespoon butter
1 tablespoon liquid sweetener
2 mangoes, peeled, pitted, and chopped
3 oranges
3 tablespoons Grand Marnier (optional)
¼ cup shelled, coarsely chopped pistachios

Per serving: Calories 448, Protein 14 g, Fat 13 g, Carbohydrates 65 g

Hopi Blue Corn Cakes

Yield: 4 servings

Corn of many colors was, and still is, an integral part of the Native American diet, culture, and religion. Many of the foods we now enjoy were first developed by Native Americans

¾ cup blue cornmeal
¾ cup whole wheat pastry flour
1 tablespoon baking powder
Egg replacer equivalent to 2 eggs,
  p. 24, or 1 ripe banana, mashed
2 tablespoons canola oil
Enough soymilk or rice milk to
  make a smooth batter

In a large bowl, mix together all the dry ingredients. Add the wet ingredients and mix them together gently until everything is moistened. Bake according to the pancake tips on page 38, but be careful turning them, as they are sometimes a little more crumbly than all-wheat pancakes. Enjoy!

Per serving: Calories 263, Protein 7 g, Fat 9 g, Carbohydrates 39 g

Ol' Timers Flannel Cakes

Yield: 4 servings

These are so named, as the story goes, because their rough texture reminded the old prospectors of their flannel shirts. This is one of my all-time favorite pancake recipes.

3 slices stale or toasted whole-
  grain bread
2 tablespoons cold-pressed canola
  oil
½ cup scalded skim milk, soymilk,
  or rice milk
1 teaspoon baking soda
⅔ cup whole wheat flour
Egg replacer equivalent to 2 eggs,
  p. 24, 2 free-range eggs, or 4
  egg whites
1 teaspoon sorghum or unsulfured
  molasses
1 teaspoon grated lemon rind

Crumble the bread in a large bowl. Combine the oil and milk, and pour over the bread. Let stand about 5 minutes, or until the milk is absorbed.

Meanwhile, mix the baking soda and flour together. Add the egg replacer, molasses, and lemon rind, and stir until uniform.

Add the second mixture to the softened bread crumbs, and stir gently. Bake according to the pancake tips on page 38. Serve hot with molasses or Apple-Ginger Syrup, page 41. Enjoy!

VARIATIONS
Try orange rind in place of lemon rind.
Use buttermilk or sour milk in place of scalded milk.

Per serving: Calories 182, Protein 5 g, Fat 8 g, Carbohydrates 22 g

Apple-Ginger Syrup

Yield: 2 cups

A delicious syrup for pancakes, and a great topping for gingerbread, poached fruit, and dairy or nondairy ice cream.

Whisk all the ingredients together in a small saucepan, and warm slowly over medium heat, stirring constantly until thick and smooth. Enjoy!

VARIATIONS

Substitute peach nectar or lemonade for apple juice concentrate and water.

Use cinnamon in place of the ginger.

1 cup thawed apple juice
   concentrate
½ cup water
½ cup arrowroot or cornstarch
½ teaspoon ginger juice,* or 1 to
   1½ teaspoons powdered ginger

*You can use powdered ginger in this recipe, but fresh ginger juice is much tastier. To make ginger juice, simply grate a piece of fresh ginger-root on a hand-held grater (don't bother to peel it). Place the grated ginger in the palm of your hand, and squeeze. You'll be amazed at how much juice is in those gingerroots! And this way you don't have to worry about pieces of the pulp in your dish. Just put it in the compost.

Per ¼ cup: Calories 44, Protein 0 g, Fat 0 g, Carbohydrates 11 g

The Art of Cooking: Sourdough

MAKING THE STARTER

In the Old West, a solitary prospector or herder couldn't go to the market when he needed yeast for his baking, so he carried along a sponge of sourdough starter. It really was "sour dough" and would keep without refrigeration forever, if used regularly. The flavor of sourdough will vary from starter to starter, and even from time to time, but is generally light and earthy with a slightly sour flavor imparted by the yeast. Even today the Western art of sourdough cookery provides one of the supreme treats for both cook and diner.

There are many ways to make your sourdough starter. In fact, a newspaper editor once asked readers to send in their recipes for making sourdough starter and got over a hundred different responses. Here are two:

1) Combine 1 tablespoon active dry yeast, 2½ cups warm water, and 2½ cups whole wheat flour (2 teaspoons honey is optional). Let set on a kitchen counter for about 5 days, stirring daily. The mixture should be somewhat bubbly and have a yeasty, "beer" aroma.

2) Let about 2½ cups milk or soymilk set outside for 4 to 5 days, lightly covered with cheesecloth. It will gather wild yeast from the air as it sours. Mix in 2½ cups whole wheat flour, and let set on your kitchen counter for 5 days as in method 1.

THE CARE AND FEEDING OF YOUR STARTER

Every time you use your starter, "feed" or replenish it with equal amounts of flour and milk or water. (I generally use soymilk as I notice a creamier flavor and texture to my pancakes.) Let it stand at room temperature for a few hours, or until it gets full of bubbles again. Then cover loosely and store in the refrigerator. A widemouth mason jar works well for storing your starter, as the large opening makes for easier stirring. I generally place a small plastic bag loosely over the mouth of the jar. Do not store your starter in a metal bowl or leave a metal spoon in it as the acids in the starter will react with the metal. If a black liquid forms on top, just pour it off. Every now and then you may also need to scrape a little mold off the top where it dries out a bit. This doesn't hurt the starter at all.

Your starter works best if it is used about once a week. If you don't use it for 2 to 3 weeks, discard about half and feed it as described above. If you don't use it for some time and it looks particularly nasty, salvage about a tablespoon of the best looking portion, feed it, and store it in a new jar. It's actually difficult to kill your starter, and it really improves with age, becoming smoother and mellower. Some sourdough aficionados put their starters in their wills to pass down from generation to generation. My starter is now about 23 years old and getting better all the time.

The starter may also be frozen if you don't think you'll use it for a while, but leave it out at room temperature for 36 hours before using it again.

PASS IT ON!

Part of the joy of the art of sourdough is being able to share it with other cooks. Simply take some of the established starter, and mix it in somewhat equal amounts with flour and milk or water. Let it set at room temperature for a few hours. Lightly cover it and give it to a friend. Please—also let them know about the care and feeding of sourdough so they don't become discouraged by not knowing what to do with it. Be generous and loving (and put some of that love in every batch of starter you give away). Pass it on, sort of like a modern, sourdough-version of "Johnny Appleseed."

Sourdough Pancakes

Yield: 4 servings

One of the great rewards of making your own sourdough starter is that you can prepare and enjoy sourdough pancakes. It's very simple to make these light, slightly chewy pancakes, but you should begin the night before.

In a large ceramic or glass bowl, gently mix the starter, milk, and flour. (The amount of flour you use is determined by the consistency you like.) Leave overnight at room temperature. Do not leave a metal spoon in the bowl; it reacts with the acid in the starter and will discolor the batter and give it a metallic flavor. This does not apply to the skillet, as it will not come into contact with the batter long enough to cause a reaction. Cast-iron or stainless steel works well.

Next morning, add the eggs or replacer, sweetener, baking soda, and oil. Mix well but don't beat. (Treat all pancake batters gently.) Cook according to the tips on page 38. Serve and enjoy!

VARIATIONS

Add ½ cup chopped nuts, fruit, or granola and/or gently mix in a pinch of cinnamon.

½ cup sourdough starter
2 cups skim milk, rice milk, or soymilk
1¾ to 2 cups whole wheat flour
2 free-range eggs (or 4 egg whites), or egg replacer equivalent to 2 eggs, p. 24*
2 tablespoons raw honey, brown rice syrup, or molasses
1 teaspoon baking soda
1 teaspoon canola oil

*It's very simple to simply eliminate the eggs altogether, as the sourdough is already very elastic.

DON'T FORGET TO FEED YOUR STARTER FOR NEXT TIME!

Per serving: Calories 333, Protein 15 g, Fat 6 g, Carbohydrates 54 g

Fruit Conserves

Yield: 2 cups

Light and not overly sweet, this can be thinned down to go over pancakes and waffles or can be thickened to make a nice jam for toast. This freezes well also.

1½ cups frozen fruit (strawberries, raspberries, peaches, etc.)
½ cup thawed frozen fruit juice concentrate
⅓ cup cornstarch or arrowroot

In a medium saucepan, cook the fruit 5 to 10 minutes, or until soft and juicy. In another bowl, dissolve the cornstarch or arrowroot in the fruit juice concentrate. Add a little of the hot fruit liquid to the concentrate, and mix well. Add this mixture to the fruit, and continue cooking over low heat until it becomes as thick as you desire. Serve and enjoy!

VARIATIONS

You can make this with fresh fruit by cooking the fruit with a small amount of water or fruit juice, then follow the remaining directions.

If using bananas or apples, add a little lemon juice to prevent it from turning brown.

Per tablespoon: Calories 14, Protein 0 g, Fat 0 g, Carbohydrates 3 g

Potatoes
Papas

Yield: 6 to 8 servings

Place a heavy skillet over medium-high heat, then add the oil. When the oil is hot, add the potatoes and cook until brown on the bottom. Turn with a spatula. Add the onions and cook until browned again. Continue cooking until the mixture is browned on all sides and cooked all the way through.

Add the remaining vegetables and seasonings. Cook another 5 to 10 minutes, or until hot and cooked throughout. Serve hot with salsa and scrambled tofu. Enjoy!

VARIATIONS

Add other chopped vegetables—celery, broccoli, etc. Add raw vegetables at the beginning and left-over cooked vegetables for the last 10 minutes of cooking.

Add any other spices that sound good to you. White pepper, crushed red pepper or cayenne, thyme, or marjoram all work well.

Add your favorite low-fat dairy or soy cheese at the end, and cook another 5 minutes.

For great Tex-Mex Fries, add 1 ripe, chopped tomato, ¼ cup minced cilantro, and roasted, peeled, and chopped chiles to taste. At the end, add 1 cup grated cheddar or soy cheddar cheese, and cook 5 more minutes. Serve with corn tortillas, salsa, Tofu Sour Cream, page 96, and/or Guacamole, page 94.

2 to 3 tablespoons cold-pressed canola oil or extra-virgin olive oil

4 large, unpeeled potatoes, partially baked and cubed

1 cup diced onions

1 red or green bell pepper, diced

½ cup sliced mushrooms

2 to 3 cloves garlic, minced

1 teaspoon chili powder

1 teaspoon dill weed (optional)

Vegetable seasoning, to taste

Per serving: Calories 139, Protein 2 g, Fat 5 g, Carbohydrates 22 g

"Sausage" Patties

Yield: 4 to 6 servings

Try these with pancakes or waffles. They're very light and tasty.

½ teaspoon sage
Pinch of black pepper
Pinch of fennel
Pinch of chili powder
Pinch of cayenne (optional)
Vegetable seasoning, to taste
Toasted sesame oil for frying
½ cup cooked adzuki beans
¼ cup finely minced onion
2 to 4 cloves garlic, minced
1 teaspoon tamari
1 cup cooked brown rice or barley

In a large bowl, mash all the ingredients together with a potato masher, except the rice or barley. Mix in the rice and form into patties. Fry in a heavy skillet with a little toasted sesame oil over medium heat until the patties are browned and heated through, turning once. Serve and enjoy!

VARIATIONS

Instead of adzuki beans, try pinto, kidney, black, or anasazi beans.

Finely chopped celery, mushrooms, or grated carrots add flavor, nutrition, and interest.

Per serving: Calories 81, Protein 3 g, Fat 0 g, Carbohydrates 17 g

Sedona Scrambled Tofu

Yield: 2 servings

This is a marvelous way to enjoy your eggs without actually eating them. It's also just plain delicious.

Place a skillet over medium heat, add the oil, and lightly sauté the scallion until tender.

Add the remaining ingredients and reduce the heat to low. Cook uncovered for 5 to 10 minutes. Serve with tortillas and beans, and garnish with sprouts and diced tomatoes or salsa. Enjoy!

VARIATIONS

Add other vegetables—zucchini, peas, corn, sunflower sprouts, etc.

1 teaspoon cold-pressed canola oil or extra-virgin olive oil
1 scallion, chopped, or ¼ cup chopped onions
1 tomato, chopped
Green chiles, chopped, to taste
½ red or green bell pepper, diced
2 to 3 cloves garlic, minced
1½ cups crumbled firm tofu, drained
Pinch of turmeric
Dash of white pepper
Dash of tamari
1 teaspoon finely minced fresh cilantro
¾ cup grated part-skim or soy mozzarella (optional)

Per serving: Calories 184, Protein 14 g, Fat 9 g, Carbohydrates 8 g

BREAKFAST BEANS

Beans are to Southwestern cuisine what grits are to Dixie. They go quite well with scrambled tofu, such as Sedona Scrambled Tofu (above), Tofu Rancheros, page 48, and Ranch Fries, page 151. Simply make extra when you're making Frijoles, page 150, keep the extra in the refrigerator (usually up to a week), or freeze in freezer bags for later use. I generally have a big bowl of frijoles in the refrigerator from which I can prepare beans for breakfast, a dip with chips, a burro for a snack, or use as an ingredient for a casserole or a side dish with dinner.

Tofu Rancheros

Yield: 2 servings

1 recipe Sedona Scrambled Tofu,
  p. 47
1 cup Frijoles, p. 150
4 yellow corn or blue corn tortillas
½ cup grated dairy or soy cheddar
  cheese
Salsa, to taste

If they're not already hot, heat the Scrambled Tofu and the Frijoles separately.

Place 2 tortillas on each plate, side by side, and evenly layer with tofu, beans, grated cheese, and salsa. You can either eat these with a knife and fork, or roll them up and eat by hand. Enjoy!

VARIATIONS

A dollop of soy yogurt or Tofu Sour Cream, page 96, a little guacamole or avocado slices, chopped lettuce or cabbage, sautéed mushrooms, chopped onion or tomatoes, crumbled feta, diced chiles, a few sprouts—get creative!

Per serving: Calories 545, Protein 31 g, Fat 20 g, Carbohydrates 55 g

Blue Corn-Maple Porridge

Yield: 6 servings

Many Native American tribes in the Southwest relied on blue corn as a staple food. This thick, sweet porridge is wonderfully tasty and satisfying on a cool morning, and very simple to prepare!

4 cups water
2 cups blue cornmeal
Maple syrup, to taste
Skim milk, soymilk, or rice milk,
  to taste

In a large saucepan, bring the water to a boil, and slowly stir in the blue cornmeal. Reduce the heat to a low boil, and cook, stirring often, until the mixture becomes thick and creamy. Add maple syrup and your favorite milk to taste. Enjoy!

Per serving: Calories 217, Protein 4 g, Fat 0 g, Carbohydrates 48 g

APPETIZERS

Jicama Fresca

Yield: 4 servings

Jicama is a tuber common to Mexico. Sweet, crunchy, and delicious, it looks somewhat like a potato before it is peeled to reveal a highly nutritious white vegetable. It is usually served raw but may be cooked (it stays crunchy). Here's a traditional way to serve it as a refreshing appetizer.

1 large jicama, peeled and cut into julienne strips
1 cup shredded lettuce
1 lime, cut into 6 wedges
¼ cup mild or hot chili powder

Arrange the jicama on a plate of shredded lettuce. Place the lime wedges around the plate, and place the chili powder in a small bowl in the center of the plate. The jicama is eaten by squeezing a little lime juice on it and dipping it in the chili powder. Enjoy!

Note: Slice the jicama with a crinkle-cutter if you have one.

Jicama Fresca is delicious with Shiitake and Sun-Dried Tomato Quesadillas, page 34, served as appetizers

Per serving: Calories 32, Protein 1 g, Fat 0 g, Carbohydrates 7 g

Nachos

Yield: 5 to 6 servings

This delicious snack or party food bears no resemblance to the fast-food served at movie theaters, malls, and sporting events. These are great!

Leave the oven hot from baking the tortilla chips. Sprinkle the chips with the cheese, chiles, and, if desired, frijoles. Pop the chips back into the oven, and bake them until the cheese is melted and bubbly, about 10 minutes. Serve hot and enjoy!

1 recipe freshly baked Tortilla Chips, p. 54
1 cup grated cheddar, Monterey Jack, or soy jalapeño cheese
Mild or hot fresh chiles, roasted, peeled, and minced, to taste
½ cup Frijoles, p. 150 (optional)

Per serving: Calories 208, Protein 10 g, Fat 7 g, Carbohydrates 24 g

Pumpkin Seeds
Pepitos

Yield: 1 cup

A very simple appetizer or a nutritious snack, try them also as a crunchy addition to salads—sort of a Southwestern crouton!

Heat a large, heavy skillet over medium heat, and add the raw pumpkin seeds. Stir often or shake the skillet to keep the seeds from sticking and burning. As they toast they will begin to pop. When most of the seeds have popped and are nicely browned and toasted, remove them from the heat, and add the tamari and seasonings. Stir to coat. Serve and enjoy!

1 cup raw pumpkin seeds, shelled
1 teaspoon tamari
½ teaspoon chili powder
Pinch of garlic powder (optional)

Per tablespoon: Calories 18, Protein 1 g, Fat 1 g, Carbohydrates 2 g

Spicy Tamari Sunnies

Yield: 2 cups

Delicious as an appetizer or snack or sprinkled as a garnish on salads and casseroles.

2 cups raw, shelled sunflower seeds
1 tablespoon tamari
½ teaspoon chili powder

Toast the sunflower seeds in a large, heavy skillet over medium heat, stirring often, until lightly browned and toasted. Remove from the heat and toss with the tamari and chili powder. Enjoy!

Per tablespoon: Calories 54, Protein 2 g, Fat 4 g, Carbohydrates 2 g

Stuffed Medjool Dates

Yield: 6 servings

Date palms grow well in the Southwestern desert and the medjool date is one of the largest and sweetest dates—perfect for stuffing.

Carefully remove the pits from the dates, and stuff with about 1 teaspoon nut butter and 1 raw almond. Serve and enjoy!

24 large medjool dates
1 cup peanut or cashew butter
24 whole, raw almonds

VARIATIONS

Substitute tahini in place of the nut butter, and raisins or currants in place of the almonds.

Per serving: Calories 370, Protein 13 g, Fat 21 g, Carbohydrates 32 g

Tortilla Chips

Yield: 5 to 6

Much better than the commercial variety, they're baked, not fried. They're also very simple to make. Wait until you've tried them hot out of the oven. Serve with salsa, bean dip, and/or guacamole.

10 to 12 yellow corn or blue corn
    tortillas
Chili powder, salt-free vegetable
    seasoning, etc., to taste

Preheat the oven to 375°F.

Cut the tortillas into 6 wedges, like a pie. You can stack them up and cut 4 or 5 at a time. Spread them out on a dry baking sheet, and sprinkle with the seasonings. Bake 7 to 10 minutes or until very crispy. Be careful not to burn them. Serve with salsa or guacamole. Enjoy!

Per serving: Calories 130, Protein 4 g, Fat 2 g, Carbohydrates 24 g

SOUPS

Ahimsa Chili

Yield: 8 servings

The term "ahimsa" means, roughly translated, "peace to all living beings." Therefore, this chili is made without ground beef and really doesn't lack anything in flavor or texture for the omission. Like most any soup or stew, the longer it cooks or the more it's reheated, the richer the flavor gets. It also freezes very well—in fact, the flavor even seems to improve. This is truly one of the best chilies I've tasted. Don't let the amount of ingredients scare you. This is actually a very easy soup to make, especially in a crock-pot.

2 cups meat substitute* (optional)

2 onions, chopped

10 to 12 tomatoes, chopped

Mild, medium, hot, or incendiary
    chiles (your choice)

3 cups sliced mushrooms (I suggest
    shiitakes.)

2 cups diced zucchini

1 red or green bell pepper, diced

1 cup low-sodium tomato purée

2 tablespoons chili powder

2 tablespoons cumin powder

Pinch of cayenne (optional)

¼ teaspoon crushed red pepper

Pinch of ground cloves

3 to 4 cloves garlic, minced

2 cups beer (imported Mexican
    beer adds the best flavor), or 1
    cup unfiltered apple juice

3 cups cooked kidney, pinto, black,
    or anasazi beans

*Tempeh, crumbled extra-firm tofu, "ground beef" or "chunky beef" textured vegetable protein, or seitan (pages 17-19) all work very well, but are not essential for a great chili.

Put all the ingredients into a large, heavy pot or crock-pot, and bring to a boil. Reduce the heat to a simmer, and cook at least 1 hour (longer for a crock-pot; refer to the manufacturer's directions). Cooking the chili for 2 to 3 hours is even better. Serve with Roasted Corn and Chili Corn Bread, page 103. Enjoy!

VARIATIONS

Try adding other vegetables to the pot—perhaps some corn, yellow squash, tomatillos, or sun-dried tomatoes.

A little minced fresh, cilantro, either in the chili or as a garnish, is also delicious.

It's nice to eat a meal and not have to worry about what your food may have died of.
    —Dr. J. H. Kellog

Per serving: Calories 174, Protein 7 g, Fat 0 g, Carbohydrates 30 g

Chile-Corn Chowder

Yield: 6 servings

Thick and creamy, this hearty chowder will satisfy the hungriest appetite, especially when accompanied by hot muffins. You can freeze it, but, it will not be as creamy when reheated.

In a large pot or soup kettle, combine all the ingredients except the soymilk or rice milk, cheese, and cilantro. Cook uncovered about 30 minutes, or until all of the vegetables are tender. Add the milk and cheese, and cook another 10 minutes, or until it begins to thicken up.

VARIATIONS

You can add bell peppers, mushrooms, zucchini or any other squash, and a half cup of black or red beans.

4 cups vegetable stock
1 onion, chopped
2 tomatoes, chopped
2 potatoes, chopped
1 carrot, diced
1 stalk celery, minced
2 to 3 cloves garlic, minced
1 cup frozen or fresh corn, cut
  from the cob
¼ cup chopped mild chiles
½ cup arrowroot or cornstarch,
  dissolved in ½ cup soymilk or
  rice milk
½ teaspoon cumin powder
½ teaspoon chili powder
Cayenne or hot sauce, to taste

1 cup soymilk or rice milk
1 cup grated soy cheddar or
  jalapeño Jack cheese (optional)
¼ cup minced fresh cilantro for
  garnish

Per serving: Calories 139, Protein 3 g, Fat 1 g, Carbohydrates 30 g

Chilled Mint-Mango-Melon Soup

Yield: 4 servings

No cooking involved! Perfect for a hot summer day. It is also refreshing poured over frozen dessert.

2 cups peeled and seeded fresh mangoes
2 cups seeded honeydew, cantaloupe, or other melon
½ cup unfiltered apple juice
2 tablespoons chopped fresh mint leaves
1 teaspoon lime juice
½ teaspoon pure vanilla extract

In a blender or food processor, blend all the ingredients together briefly. (Leave them slightly chunky, if you prefer.) Place in the freezer for about an hour, or until icy but not quite frozen. (If you would like to serve it later, freeze completely and then thaw about ¾ of the way before serving.) Garnish with a dollop of dairy or soy yogurt and a fresh mint leaf. Enjoy!

VARIATIONS

Try other fruits or a combination of fruits— peaches, raspberries, strawberries, papaya, blueberries, pears, etc. You're only limited by your imagination.

Per serving: Calories 99, Protein 1 g, Fat 0 g, Carbohydrates 23 g

Cilantro Soup
Sopa de Cilantro

Yield: 6 servings

A great beginning to a Southwestern fiesta or a nice light meal served with a crusty French bread.

Cook the potatoes in the stock over medium heat about 15 minutes, or until fork-tender.

Remove from the heat and stir in everything except the lemon juice. In a food processor or blender, purée the soup in small batches until smooth. Stir in the lemon juice, and serve immediately, perhaps garnished with a cilantro leaf and a little lemon zest. Enjoy!

6 medium russet potatoes, cut into 1-inch cubes
6 cups vegetable stock
2 to 3 cloves garlic, minced
1 cup cilantro leaves
Hot sauce, to taste
Juice of 2 lemons

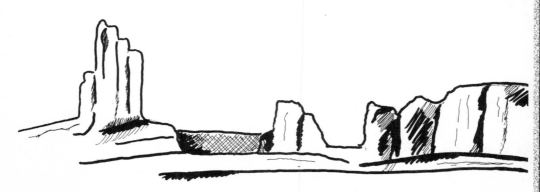

Gazpacho

Yield: 8 servings

This is the perfect soup for a hot summer day—no cooking needed! Traditionally gazpacho is a chilled vegetable soup with a spicy Southwestern accent. Feel free to experiment to suit your tastes.

2 cucumbers, peeled (optional) and diced*

1 medium red onion, diced

4 large tomatoes, chopped (peeled and seeded, if preferred)

1 large green or red bell pepper, diced

1 to 2 cloves garlic, minced

Juice of 3 limes

4 cups low-sodium tomato, V-8, or other vegetable juice

3 tablespoons minced fresh cilantro

*If you use European cucumbers (the long ones found wrapped in plastic in supermarkets), there is no need to peel them. They're considered "burpless" and they generally haven't been waxed or sprayed.

Mix everything together in a large bowl, and refrigerate several hours or overnight to let the flavors marry. Serve in a chilled mug or bowl with baked tortilla chips. Garnish, if desired, with a little extra cilantro. (Always keep a little salsa or Tabasco on hand for the more adventurous.) Enjoy!

To peel tomatoes, cut a small "X" in the blossom end (the opposite end from the stem). Place the tomato in a hot steamer basket or boiling water for 20 to 30 seconds, then plunge into cold water for another 20 seconds. The peel will remove very easily.

To remove the seeds from the tomatoes, cut the tomato in half, crosswise. Squeeze the tomato gently to loosen the seeds, hold the tomato firmly, and snap it with your wrist over a trash can. All the tomato seeds will come out with just a couple of snaps. If you have trouble at first, practice. It will come to you. It's much simpler than trying to remove the seeds with a spoon or knife.

Per serving: Calories 54, Protein 1 g, Fat 0 g, Carbohydrates 11 g

Mission Lentils

Yield: 6 servings

It's easy to imagine the inhabitants of a California monastery in the days of "Old California" gathering for an evening meal of this hearty, delicious soup. Serve with corn bread or muffins and a salad.

In a large, heavy pot or Dutch oven, cook the lentils in the vegetable stock until tender but not mushy, about 35 to 40 minutes. Add the vegetables, wine, and a bay leaf, and continue cooking until the vegetables are tender and the soup begins to thicken. Place ⅓ cup crumbled feta in each bowl, and fill with hot soup. Sprinkle with parsley or cilantro. Enjoy!

VARIATIONS

Shiitake, button, portobello, or chanterelle mushrooms are wonderful in this, as well as zucchini, corn, bell peppers, or sun-dried tomatoes, soaked and chopped.

Spice it with fresh, chopped chiles.

Add other seasonings—cumin powder, oregano, or fennel.

2 cups uncooked lentils
2 cups unsalted vegetable stock
1 small onion, diced
2 to 3 cloves garlic, minced
2 stalks celery, minced
1 carrot, grated or diced
4 to 5 tomatoes, chopped
1 cup burgundy wine
1 bay leaf
2 cups crumbled feta cheese
½ cup minced fresh parsley or
  cilantro

Per serving: Calories 476, Protein 25 g, Fat 16 g, Carbohydrates 46 g

Onion Soup Veracruz

Yield: 6 servings

Traditionally made with beef stock, this rich and elegant soup is really improved by the use of miso. Serve this as the beginning course to a dinner party, and see how many people ask for the recipe. (Have it handy.) This soup freezes well.

1 to 1½ pounds peeled onions (Try Vidalia or Maui onions when they're in season.)

2 tablespoons toasted sesame oil

1 red and 1 green bell pepper, sliced in thin julienne strips

2 tablespoons whole wheat flour

2 bay leaves

½ teaspoon chili powder

¼ teaspoon freshly ground black pepper (optional)

Salt-free vegetable seasoning, to taste

Approximately 6 cups vegetable stock

2 tablespoons dark miso

6 slices whole grain French bread (optional)

½ cup grated dairy or soy Monterey Jack or cheddar cheese (optional)

¼ cup minced fresh cilantro (optional)

Cut the onions in half crosswise, then slice thinly with the grain. Heat a large, heavy pot, then add the sesame oil. Sauté the onions slowly over medium heat, stirring frequently until very tender, about 15 to 20 minutes. Add the bell peppers and sauté another 5 minutes. Add the flour, bay leaves, chili powder, black pepper and vegetable seasoning, mix well, and cook for about 5 minutes, stirring constantly.

Slowly add the vegetable stock a little at a time, and continue to stir, letting it thicken slightly before adding more stock. Cover and simmer for at least ½ hour. Reduce the heat to very low; once it stops boiling, add the miso, then mix in thoroughly, and serve.

To serve traditionally, put the soup into ovenproof serving bowls, top each with a slice of bread and a sprinkle of cheese, and place under a hot broiler until the cheese melts and browns slightly. Serve bubbly hot. Enjoy!

VARIATIONS

Though not needed with all that onion, a little garlic adds a nice touch. A dash of tamari or Dr. Bronner's Mineral Bouillon adds a little of the salty flavor associated with onion soup.

Per serving: Calories 113, Protein 3 g, Fat 5 g, Carbohydrates 12 g

Peanut Soup

Yield: 4 servings

This is a very rich soup and goes best with a light entrée.

In a large, heavy pot, melt the butter and sauté the onion until just brown. Whisk in the flour and seasonings, stir, and cook over medium heat for just a few minutes. Stir in the peanut butter and milk, and cook, stirring until smooth and thickened slightly. Garnish with the almond slivers, serve, and enjoy!

VARIATIONS

You can use cashew butter, almond butter, even macadamia butter instead of peanut butter.

1 tablespoon butter, margarine, or canola oil
¼ cup chopped onion
1 tablespoon whole wheat pastry flour
¼ teaspoon mace
¼ teaspoon dried basil
¼ teaspoon grated lemon rind
¼ teaspoon minced cilantro
Freshly ground black pepper, to taste
⅓ cup natural peanut butter
2 cups soymilk or rice milk
¼ cup slivered almonds

Per serving: Calories 257, Protein 11 g, Fat 19 g, Carbohydrates 11 g

Pumpkin Stew

Yield: 8 to 10 servings

A delicious, hearty soup your family will really enjoy on a brisk autumn evening. For a festive occasion, scrub and hollow out an extra pumpkin, and use it as an unusual serving bowl.

1 medium pumpkin, seeded, peeled, and chopped
1 red or green bell pepper, diced
1 onion, chopped
1 cup fresh corn, cut from the cob
1 cup cooked anasazi or tepary beans
¼ cup sunflower seeds
Fresh cilantro, for garnish

In a large pot, combine all the ingredients, except the cilantro, and add fresh cold water just to cover. Bring to a boil and then reduce to a simmer. Cover and cook for 40 minutes, or until all the vegetables are tender. Pour into a large serving bowl or hollowed pumpkin. Garnish with cilantro and serve with hot corn muffins. Enjoy!

VARIATIONS

Other squash will work well—Hubbard, butternut, etc.

If seasoning is desired, cilantro, fresh mild chiles, or ground cumin seeds will add a nice touch, as well as a touch of salt, tamari, or salt-free seasoning.

Illegal aliens have always been a problem in the United States. Ask any Indian.

—Robert Orben

Per serving: Calories 128, Protein 4 g, Fat 1 g, Carbohydrates 22 g

Rattlesnake Chili

Yield: 8 servings

No, there is no rattlesnake meat in this. It was named for the type of bean I used—rattlesnake beans—the first time I made this. Pintos, kidneys, black turtles, anasazis, and teparies also work well.

Mix all the ingredients together in a large pot or crock pot, and cook about an hour or longer, the longer the better. Serve with corn bread or tortillas and, perhaps, a little grated low-fat dairy or soy cheese. Enjoy!

VARIATIONS

Add chopped zucchini or yellow squash, chopped cooked potatoes, or
mushrooms. For something deliciously different, try serving this over a baked potato.

3 cups cooked beans
1 onion, chopped
1 sweet red or green bell pepper, chopped
2 ears of corn, cut from the cob, or 1 (10-ounce) package frozen corn
3 tomatoes, chopped
1 (6-ounce) can tomato sauce
3 to 4 cloves garlic, minced
2 mild or hot chiles, roasted, peeled, and minced
2 tablespoons chili powder
1 tablespoon cumin powder
1 teaspoon epazote
2 tablespoons minced fresh cilantro
Pinch of ground cloves
Salt or vegetable seasoning, to taste
1 bottle beer (optional)
Juice of 1 lime

I only wish I had time for one more bowl of chili.
—Allegedly, the dying words of Kit Carson

Per serving: Calories 149, Protein 6 g, Fat 0 g, Carbohydrates 30 g

Southwest Black Bean Soup

Yield: 6 servings

This is my favorite version of black bean soup. The orange juice and pulp really add a nice touch. As with any bean soup, a crock-pot can really make it a simple operation. This soup freezes wonderfully.

2 cups dry black beans (turtle beans)
1 tablespoon extra-virgin olive oil (optional)
1 onion, chopped
2 stalks celery, minced
1 carrot, diced
3 to 4 cloves garlic, minced
1 fresh green chile, roasted, peeled, and minced
1 tablespoon chili powder
1 tablespoon cumin powder
1 tablespoon minced fresh cilantro
Salt-free vegetable seasoning, to taste

1 teaspoon tamari
Juice of 2 limes or 1 lemon
Juice of 1 orange with just a little of the orange pulp

Pick through the dry beans, discarding any rocks, field corn, shrivelled beans, etc. Soak the beans in plenty of water overnight (preferably at least 8 hours). Pour off the soaking water, and cover the beans with fresh water about ½ inch above the beans. Add the vegetables, chili powder, cumin, cilantro, and salt-free vegetable seasoning. Cook for 1 to 1½ hours over medium heat, or until the beans are very tender. If using a crock-pot, let cook all day.

Add the tamari, lime or lemon juice, and orange juice and pulp. Cook uncovered about 30 more minutes. Garnish with a dollop of nonfat yogurt and a fresh cilantro leaf. Serve hot with Roasted Corn and Chili Corn Bread, page 103. Enjoy!

Note: Although it's not absolutely necessary to soak beans before cooking them, it does help. First, it cuts down on the cooking time by quite a bit. Secondly it makes them more digestible. All beans except lentils and split peas should be soaked.

Per serving: Calories 225, Protein 12 g, Fat 0 g, Carbohydrates 43 g

Summer Greens Bisque

Yield: 4 servings

Light and tasty, this soup is a good beginning to a meal. With a salad and roll, it becomes a meal in itself.

Combine all the ingredients, except the miso, in a large pot, and bring to a boil. Reduce the heat to a simmer, cover, and cook 30 to 40 minutes. If desired, add the miso just before serving. Serve garnished with minced parsley or cilantro and a few croutons. Enjoy!

VARIATIONS

Use other vegetables, such as chopped zucchini, sliced mushrooms (shiitake, portobello, button), artichoke hearts, leeks, finely chopped turnips or parsnips, diced celery, peas, corn, etc. Also try other herbs and seasonings, such as fresh basil or cilantro, dill, a pinch of ginger, Chinese 5-spice seasoning, and/or hot peppers.

Add cubes of tofu with the vegetables.

1 pound red chard, green chard, spinach, or other summer greens, chopped
1 small red onion, minced
1 small carrot, grated
1 tomato, chopped
2 cloves garlic, minced
4 cups vegetable stock or juice
Dash of balsamic vinegar
Dash of tamari
Salt-free vegetable seasoning, to taste
1 tablespoon light miso (optional)

Per serving: Calories 60, Protein 3 g, Fat 0 g, Carbohydrates 8 g

Todo En La Caldera

Yield: 8 servings

Literally, "all in the pot," this wonderful, spicy-as-you-like-it stew has a unique south-of-the-border character. This is also a good recipe for using up leftovers or vegetables that have been around just a little too long. This soup freezes well.

1 red or green bell pepper, diced

Fresh chiles, any variety, roasted, peeled, and minced, to taste

2 tablespoons extra-virgin olive oil

3 to 4 cloves garlic, minced

1 large onion, chopped

2 medium zucchini, chopped

1 cup corn, cut fresh from the cob

5 to 6 ripe tomatoes, chopped

1 teaspoon chili powder

1 teaspoon cumin powder

2 tablespoons minced fresh parsley or cilantro

Juice of 2 limes

Salt-free vegetable seasoning, to taste

Vegetable stock or water, to cover

In a large, heavy pot, sauté the onion, zucchini, bell peppers, and chiles in the olive oil until tender. Add the garlic and sauté 2 to 3 minutes longer. Add the rest of the ingredients and enough stock or cold water to cover. Bring to a boil, reduce the heat, and simmer about 1 hour, or cook in a crock-pot if you prefer. Serve hot with corn bread. For the more adventurous, place a bowl of salsa or Tabasco on the table. Enjoy!

VARIATIONS

You may skip the oil and braise the vegetables in a little stock or even a good imported Mexican beer. In fact, even if you use the oil, the beer will still add a nice flavor.

A little grated Monterey Jack or jalapeño soy cheese sprinkled on top makes the soup more festive.

If you can find them in your area, try chopping up a couple of tomatillos into the soup.

Beans of any variety (kidney, pinto, anasazi, etc.) make a good addition.

Hominy or posole is especially good in this soup!

Of soup and love the first is best.

—Spanish proverb

Per serving: Calories 78, Protein 1 g, Fat 2 g, Carbohydrates 10 g

Vegetarian Menudo

Yield: 8 servings

This spicy stew tastes best when you make it with dried lima beans, black-eyed peas, and posole, soaking and cooking them yourself. But if that is too time consuming, use frozen or canned ingredients. It will still be mighty good.

In a large, heavy pot, sauté or braise the onions, garlic, and chiles in the olive oil or red wine, stirring constantly, until well cooked and tender. Add the menudo spices and continue cooking. The mixture will start to stick; keep stirring and scraping everything back down into the pot, and cook for another 5 minutes. Add the tomatoes and scrape the pot to mix all the ingredients.

Add the remaining ingredients and stir well. Cook together about 30 minutes or longer. Adjust the seasonings and serve topped with some chopped raw onion. Traditionally, menudo is served with a lemon wedge (probably to cut the fat from the tripe that is traditionally used). Serve a stack of hot tortillas on the side, and enjoy!

2 large red or yellow onions, chopped

3 to 4 cloves garlic, minced

Hot chiles, roasted, peeled, and minced, to taste

¼ cup extra-virgin olive oil or red wine

3 tablespoons menudo spices (or to taste), or 2 tablespoons chili powder and 1 tablespoon ground Mexican oregano

4 large tomatoes, or 1 (28-ounce) can crushed tomatoes

2 cups cooked posole or hominy

2 cups cooked lima beans

2 cups cooked black-eyed peas

1 pound frozen corn, or kernels sliced from 3 ears of fresh corn

8 cups water or vegetable stock

*Menudo spices are a blend of ground powdered chiles, cumin, and oregano. You can find either this dried spice combination or a paste which is made by mixing the spices with a little vinegar.

Per serving: Calories 279, Protein 9g, Fat 7g, Carbohydrates 44 g

Croutons

Yield: 4 cups

4 slices whole-grain bread
Butter or olive oil
½ teaspoon garlic granules
½ teaspoon dried basil
½ teaspoon dried oregano
Pinch of black pepper
1 teaspoon dairy or soy Parmesan
   (optional)

Preheat the oven to 400°F.

Spread each slice of whole-grain bread with butter or olive oil on both sides. Cut into 1-inch cubes and place on a baking sheet.

In a small bowl, mix the herbs and cheese (if using), and sprinkle evenly on the bread cubes. Bake, tossing lightly every 5 minutes, until crispy and toasted, about 15 to 20 minutes. Serve with soups, salads, or casseroles.

Per ½ cup: Calories 43, Protein 1 g, Fat 2 g, Carbohydrates 4 g

SALADS AND DRESSINGS

Black Bean Salad with Feta and Mint

Yield: 6 servings

This is a beautiful side dish or light summer entrée with corn bread and a raw vegetable salad. Take this to potlucks!

4 cups cooked black beans
1 small red onion, finely chopped
1 small red or green bell pepper, diced
½ cup finely minced fresh mint (Save a couple of sprigs for garnish.)
2 ounces feta, crumbled (⅜ cup)
2 tablespoons extra-virgin olive oil
3 to 4 tablespoons fresh lemon or lime juice
1 to 2 cloves garlic, minced
½ teaspoon tamari
Freshly ground black pepper (optional)

Combine all the ingredients in a bowl, and mix well. Refrigerate and serve chilled.

Enjoy!

VARIATIONS

Add other vegetables for more color, taste, texture, and variety—chopped celery, carrots, cucumbers, tomatoes, mushrooms, or whole kernel corn.

For something different, add chopped oranges, mangoes, or pineapple.

Sprinkle lightly with toasted nuts or seeds—sliced almonds, pine nuts, pumpkin seeds, or sunflower seeds.

Try a little crumbled tofu in place of the feta cheese.

Substitute other beans—adzukis, small red, etc.

Use cilantro in place of the mint and perhaps just a dash of balsamic vinegar.

Per serving: Calories 230, Protein 10 g, Fat 7 g, Carbohydrates 31 g

California Lentil Salad

Yield: 6 servings

This delicious salad is good served hot or cold. It's a perfect dish for potlucks and cookouts.

Cook the lentils until just done, tender but not mushy. Drain (save the broth for a soup).

Add the rest of the ingredients, and mix together well. Serve hot or refrigerate for later. Enjoy!

VARIATIONS

Sprinkle with crumbled feta or grated Romano cheese.

Grated jicama or carrots are a nice addition.

½ pound green or brown lentils (1¼ cups)
2 stalks celery, thinly sliced
1 small red onion, diced
½ red bell pepper, diced
2 to 3 scallions or shallots, chopped
1 tomato, diced
2 to 3 cloves garlic, minced
¼ cup balsamic vinegar
⅓ cup extra-virgin olive oil
½ tablespoon Dijon mustard
¼ cup toasted walnuts

Per serving: Calories 226, Protein 6 g, Fat 14 g, Carbohydrates 18 g

Carrot and Beet Salad

Yield: 4 servings

A colorful salad with an unusual, sweet-tart flavor, this makes a nice garnish on a combination plate. The lime juice adds a very nice Southwestern touch, but you might also add a little minced cilantro and shredded jicama for a more pronounced ethnic flavor.

Gently mix the vegetables together. Don't over mix or the beets will turn everything red. You want the colors somewhat distinct.

In another small bowl, mix the dressing ingredients together and gently fold into the vegetables to moisten. Serve and enjoy, garnished perhaps with a leaf of cilantro.

1 cup grated carrots
½ cup grated beets
¼ cup shredded red onion
¼ cup apple juice concentrate
Juice of 1 lime
½ teaspoon balsamic vinegar
¼ cup Tofu Mayo, p. 96 (optional)

Per serving: Calories 53, Protein 0 g, Fat 0 g, Carbohydrates 12 g

Creamy Coleslaw

Yield: *6 servings*

This is coleslaw with a difference, a few unusual flavors that I'm sure you'll like. Serve this at your next cookout, and wait for the raves.

Coleslaw dressing:

2 tablespoons Tofu Mayonnaise, p. 96
1 teaspoon Dijon or spicy mustard
1 tablespoon apple cider or rice vinegar
1 tablespoon raw honey or brown rice syrup
1 teaspoon poppy or caraway seeds (optional)

2 cups shredded green cabbage
1 cup shredded red cabbage
½ cup grated carrot
¼ cup minced red onion
¼ cup raisins
1 red or green apple, grated

In a large bowl, mix the dressing ingredients together well. Add the rest of the ingredients, and mix well. It's best to refrigerate this at least 1 hour to let the flavors marry and to bring out all the juices. Serve and enjoy!

VARIATIONS

For an interesting touch, add shredded jicama, minced celery, or thin julienne slices of red or green bell pepper.

Try raspberry or balsamic vinegar.

Substitute a pear for the apple.

Add ½ teaspoon toasted sesame oil.

Substitute apple or pineapple juice concentrate for the honey.

Add a little dill, parsley, or cilantro.

Per serving: Calories 62, Protein 1 g, Fat 0 g, Carbohydrates 14 g

Jicama Slaw

Yield: *4 servings*

I created this on the spur-of-the-moment as a garnish to go with enchiladas, but it makes a great salad course or appetizer for a Mexican fiesta. It's also very refreshing as a side dish on a hot day.

Toss everything together well. Serve with a twist of lime peel. Enjoy!

3 cups grated jicama
1 cup finely shredded red onion
½ cup very thinly julienned red pepper
½ teaspoon chili powder
Juice of 1 lime

Per serving: Calories 54 , Protein 2 g, Fat 0 g, Carbohydrates 12 g

Southwest Potato Salad

Yield: *6 servings*

A zesty, creamy potato salad with a Southwestern flair. This salad goes great with grilled veggies and beans.

Steam the potatoes until soft and cooked throughout. In a large bowl, mix all the ingredients together, and refrigerate at least an hour before serving to let all the flavors mingle. Serve and enjoy!

VARIATIONS

Add 1 or 2 mild chiles, roasted, peeled, and minced.

Crumble a little feta cheese into the salad just before serving.

2 pounds red or white potatoes, scrubbed and cubed
1 red onion, minced
1 red and 1 green bell pepper, minced
1 to 2 cloves garlic, minced
3 tablespoons Tofu Mayonnaise, p. 96
Juice of 1 lime
Black pepper, to taste
Pinch of chile powder
Pinch of cumin
¼ cup minced fresh cilantro

Per serving: Calories 152, Protein 3 g, Fat 0 g, Carbohydrates 34 g

Taco Salad

Yield: 1 serving

Did you know that the highest calorie, highest fat item on the menu at most Mexican restaurants is the taco salad? Deep-fried shell, high-fat meat, beans fried in lard, avocado guacamole, whole-milk cheese, sour cream, and olives! Here's a delicious taco salad you can live with.

1 whole wheat flour tortilla

Small amount of oil or non-stick spray

½ cup shredded lettuce

¼ cup diced jicama

1 tomatillo, chopped

¼ cup cooked kidney or pinto beans or Frijoles, p.150

¼ cup Guacamole, p. 94

¼ cup salsa of your choice

1 tablespoon Tofu Sour Cream, p. 96

1 tablespoon grated cheddar, Monterey Jack, or soy cheddar cheese

1 cherry tomato, for garnish

Preheat the oven to 400°F.

Lightly coat an oven-proof consomme or coffee cup with oil or non-stick spray. Place the tortilla in the cup to form a bowl, and bake for 7 to 10 minutes, or until golden-brown and crispy. Let it cool and then remove the baked tortilla from the cup. This will make an edible bowl for your salad. Fill in the following order: lettuce, jicama, tomatillo, beans, guacamole, salsa, sour cream, and cheese.

From the end opposite the stem, cut the cherry tomato in quarters, being sure not to cut all the way through the bottom. Spread it out to form a flower. Place it on top of your salad. Enjoy!

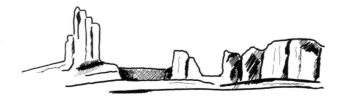

Per serving: Calories 224, Protein 9 g, Fat 5 g, Carbohydrates 33 g

Three-Bean Salad

Yield: 4 servings

A healthy variation of an old recipe I found in a cookbook from the '50s. I just brought it up to date a little and gave it a Southwest accent.

Toss everything together well and garnish, if desired, with scallion flowers or a tomato rose (see note). Serve and enjoy!

Note: To make scallion flowers, cut the root off the scallion, and cut the green off just above where it branches out. Using the white part of the scallion, cut from about 1 inch in to the white end of the scallion. Do this 4 to 5 times around the scallion. Place in a bowl of ice water for 2 to 3 hours; the cut parts will curl back like the petals of a flower.

To make a tomato rose, start at the end opposite the stem end. Cut a little flat base, then peel the tomato from the base in a spiral fashion all the way down to the core. It helps to use a very sharp paring knife and a tomato that's not too ripe. Then coil the peel back, and set it on its base. A couple of fresh basil or mint leaves coming out from the base add a nice touch.

Kiwis, lemons, limes, oranges, and plums all make very pretty roses.

VARIATIONS

Add a few mild or hot chiles, 1 cup cooked rice or other grain, a dash of chili powder, or a dash of balsamic vinegar.

Substitute other beans, even green beans.

1 cup cooked pinto beans
1 cup cooked black beans
1 cup cooked kidney beans
1 small onion or 2 scallions, chopped
1 stalk celery, minced
½ carrot, grated
1 tablespoon cider vinegar
Dash of tamari
Dash of Tabasco (optional)
2 tablespoons minced fresh cilantro or parsley

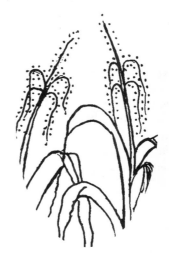

Per serving: Calories 191, Protein 10 g, Fat 0 g, Carbohydrates 36 g

Tomato-Onion-Bell Pepper Salad

Yield: 4 servings

Here's a gardener's delight. When the tomatoes ripen, generally there are bell peppers and onions that are ready to harvest. This salad can go straight from the garden to the table in 5 minutes or less.

4 large, ripe tomatoes, thinly sliced
2 onions, thinly sliced
2 medium green or red bell
   peppers, julienned

Toss all the ingredients together and serve. Enjoy!

VARIATIONS

Use a light Vinaigrette, page 82, or a little lemon or lime juice. If you planted basil with your tomatoes, you might chop a few leaves and toss them into your salad with a little minced garlic. Basil is a good companion plant that strengthens tomatoes and helps prevent tomato worms.

Per serving: Calories 60, Protein 2 g, Fat 0 g, Carbohydrates 12 g

Tomato Sun Salad

Yield: 4 servings

Here's another very simple salad with a sun theme, just for the fun and taste of it.

2 cups sunflower seed sprouts
1 cup chopped hydrated sun-dried
   tomatoes
1 cup sliced sunchokes (Jerusalem
   artichokes), steamed

Toss all the ingredients together, and serve. Enjoy!

Note: To hydrate the sun-dried tomatoes, simply cook or soak the dried tomatoes in water until they are soft and easy to cut.

VARIATION

If you would like a salad dressing with this salad, blend hydrated sun-dried tomatoes with ¼ cup of sunflower oil until smooth.

Per serving: Calories 57, Protein 2 g, Fat 0 g, Carbohydrates 11 g

Tropical Fruit Salad with Lime Marinade

Yield: 4 servings

You can make this a a few hours or a day ahead of time and keep in a tightly closed container in the refrigerator. This will give the flavors a chance to develop.

In a large bowl, gently combine the fruit, lime juice and zest, and honey or rice syrup. Marinate at least 1 hour. (Several hours would be better.) Just before serving, toss with the minced mint. Garnish with a mint sprig. Serve and enjoy!

VARIATIONS

Try with other fruits or a small amount of grated fresh coconut.

Toss in a few chopped nuts or seeds—pecans, walnuts, almonds, sunflower seeds, or sesame seeds.

Toss in a few raisins, currants, or other chopped dried fruit.

Top with a dollop of nonfat yogurt or Tofu Whipped Cream, page 170. Serve over frozen, nonfat yogurt or nondairy frozen dessert.

1 large, ripe pineapple, cubed
2 large, ripe mangoes, cubed
1 large, ripe papaya, cubed
Juice of 2 limes
½ teaspoon finely minced lime zest (green peel only)
¼ cup raw honey or brown rice syrup
3 tablespoons minced fresh mint leaves
4 fresh mint sprigs

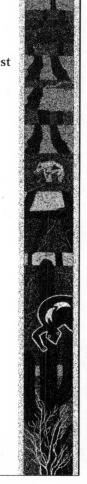

Per serving: Calories 241, Protein 1 g, Fat 0 g, Carbohydrates 56 g

White Bean and Sun-Dried Tomato Salad

Yield: 6 servings

When you think of beans and Southwestern cuisine, you generally think of pinto or kidney beans, but white beans are often used for a different flavor. I developed this recipe from a dish I was served in southern California. For a light summer meal, just serve this cold bean salad with a little corn bread and some steamed greens. Yum!

4 cups cooked navy or Great
   Northern beans
1 cup chopped hydrated sun-dried
   tomatoes
½ cup diagonally sliced shallots or
   scallions
¼ cup minced fresh cilantro
¼ cup olive oil
1 tablespoon balsamic vinegar
Freshly ground black pepper, to
   taste
Dash of tamari (optional)

Mix all the ingredients together and refrigerate to let all the flavors develop. Serve and enjoy!

VARIATIONS

Substitute black or kidney beans (or a combination of beans), and use some chopped fresh basil in place of the cilantro.

Add a clove or two of minced garlic.

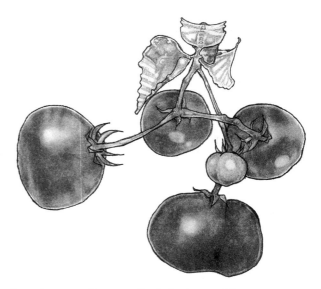

Per serving: Calories 279, Protein 10 g, Fat 9 g, Carbohydrates 38 g

Apple Mustard Dressing

Yield: about 2 cups

I developed this dressing when I could find nothing else I liked and had these ingredients on hand. It shows how imagination goes hand-in-hand with creativity. This is a very strongly flavored sweet-and-hot sauce. It can be made milder by some of the variations following it. This makes a wonderful marinade for grilled tofu or a dip for spring rolls, as well as a condiment for sandwiches.

Mix all the ingredients together well. Refrigerate until needed. Enjoy!

VARIATIONS

May be diluted with water for a milder (and thinner) dressing or for a marinade.

For a sandwich dressing, omit the water. Cut all the ingredients in half, and add 1 cup of Tofu Mayonnaise, page 96, for a mild and creamy honey mustard. This is also good on sandwiches.

1 cup apple juice concentrate, thawed and undiluted
½ cup Dijon mustard
2 tablespoons raw honey (optional)
¼ cup toasted sesame oil
¼ cup water

Per tablespoon: Calories 36, Protein 0 g, Fat 2 g, Carbohydrates 4 g

Basic Vinaigrette

Yield: about 2 cups

This can be varied to make raspberry, tarragon, balsamic, and many other varieties of vinaigrette. Here's the basic recipe and a list of delightful variations.

½ cup red wine vinegar
2 teaspoons tamari
1 tablespoon Dijon mustard
1 to 2 cloves garlic, minced
Juice of ½ lemon
1 teaspoon raw honey or brown
   rice syrup (optional)
1 cup water

Mix all the ingredients together well, and refrigerate until needed. Enjoy!

TARRAGON VINAIGRETTE
Add 1 tablespoon dried tarragon.

RASPBERRY VINAIGRETTE
Substitute raspberry vinegar for the red wine vinegar.

BALSAMIC VINAIGRETTE
Substitute balsamic vinegar for the red wine vinegar.

Per tablespoon: Calories 2, Protein 0 g, Fat 0 g, Carbohydrates 0 g

Garlic Dressing

Yield: 2 cups

If you love garlic, here is the dressing for you. If you're not all that crazy about garlic, cut back on the amount or eliminate it, and you'll still enjoy this creamy salad dressing.

1½ cups Tofu Mayonnaise, p. 96
3 to 4 cloves garlic, minced
1 scallion, chopped
Juice of 1 lemon
¼ teaspoon prepared mustard
¼ teaspoon celery seed
Dash of horseradish (optional)

Combine everything in a blender until smooth. Refrigerate until ready to serve. Enjoy!

Per tablespoon: Calories 19, Protein 0 g, Fat 2 g, Carbohydrates 0 g

Lime-Cilantro Dressing

Yield: 2 cups

A different type of salad dressing that is very refreshing and tasty.

Blend all the ingredients together well, and refrigerate. Enjoy!

VARIATIONS

Substitute parsley for the cilantro.
A chopped scallion will also add a nice touch.

1½ cups Tofu Mayonnaise, p. 96
Juice of 3 limes
1 clove garlic, finely minced
⅓ cup finely minced fresh cilantro

Per tablespoon: Calories 19, Protein 0 g, Fat 2 g, Carbohydrates 0 g

Orange-Tahini Dressing

Yield: about 2 cups

Try this on salads, of course, but also over stir-fries, burgers, potatoes, casseroles, plain rice, etc. This versatile sauce adds flavor to many dishes.

Combine everything in a blender until smooth, and refrigerate until needed. Enjoy!

VARIATIONS

Substitute ½ as much red wine vinegar or balsamic vinegar for the cider vinegar.

In place of olive oil, try toasted sesame oil.

Use peanut, almond, or cashew butter in place of all or part of the tahini.

Buttermilk will work well in place of the yogurt or tofu, but use less.

Just a pinch of cumin or cayenne adds a nice flavor.

⅓ cup cider vinegar
¼ cup extra-virgin olive oil
1 to 2 cloves garlic, minced
1 teaspoon tamari
¾ cup tahini
¼ cup lemon juice
¼ cup nonfat yogurt or soft tofu
Juice of 1 orange

Per tablespoon: Calories 51, Protein 1 g, Fat 4 g, Carbohydrates 2 g

Sesame Seed Dressing

Yield: about 2 cups

This dressing is fairly sweet; try it with fruit as well as with vegetables. You can also use it for marinades and stir-fries.

¼ cup unhulled sesame seeds
¼ cup toasted sesame oil
½ cup rice vinegar or mirin
1 cup pineapple juice

In a dry pan, roast the sesame seeds over medium heat, stirring constantly, until crispy and browned. Mix together well with the rest of the ingredients, and refrigerate. Enjoy!

VARIATIONS

Try other juices and/or other vinegars.

Per tablespoon: Calories 27, Protein 0 g, Fat 2 g, Carbohydrates 2 g

Thousand Island Dressing

Yield: about 2 cups

It's quite simple to give this traditional dressing a Southwestern flair. Just substitute a hot chile or two for some of the pickles. Try it on the Taco Salad, page 76.

½ cup non-fat yogurt
½ cup Tofu Mayonnaise, p. 96
½ cup tomato sauce
¼ cup diced sweet pickles
2 tablespoons cider vinegar
1 teaspoon raw honey or brown
  rice syrup (optional)
Juice of 1 lemon or lime

Whisk or blend everything together well. Refrigerate until ready to use. Enjoy!

Note: You can find honey-sweetened pickles in your local health food store; if you prefer them.

VARIATIONS

Substitute pickled chiles for the cucumber pickles.

Substitute marinara sauce for the tomato sauce.

Use firm tofu in place of the yogurt for a dairy-free version.

Substitute ½ as much red wine vinegar or balsamic vinegar for the cider vinegar.

Per tablespoon: Calories 8, Protein 0 g, Fat 0 g, Carbohydrates 2 g

SAUCES AND SALSAS

About Dairy-Free Cheese and Cream Sauces

I once tried to question a very tradition-oriented chef as to why he never tried to make his white sauce with oil and whole wheat pastry flour instead of butter and white flour. Very exasperated at my impertinence, he explained scientifically the different properties of each ingredient and how it was "impossible, it just won't work." Now I don't consider myself a miracle worker, but several times since then I've performed the "impossible," as I always make my sauces with oil instead of butter or margarine and generally use whole wheat pastry flour instead of all-purpose white flour. They come out delicious. I believe that if we think something is impossible it will be, and the opposite, it follows, is just as true. Nothing, then, is impossible. (Of course, if you make a white sauce with whole wheat pastry flour, I concede that, to be accurate, you will have to call it an off-white sauce.)

Basic Off-White Sauce

Yield: about 2 cups

This is the base for many other sauces and dishes. The whole trick is in making the roux.

2 tablespoons cold-pressed canola oil
2 tablespoons whole wheat pastry flour
Approximately 2 cups skim milk, soymilk, or rice milk

Put the oil into a preheated heavy skillet or saucepan. Add the flour and stir well until you get a thick paste that somewhat resembles dry mashed potatoes. This is the roux. You may have to adjust and add more oil or flour, as needed. Do not cook too long or let the flour get too brown. Slowly add the milk, stirring with a wire whisk constantly. As the sauce thickens, add a little more milk until you have about 2 cups and it has reached the thickness or consistency you desire. If at any stage it becomes too lumpy, just have a go at it with the wire whisk until the sauce becomes smooth. (Hold it like a pencil, not a chisel, and make figure 8s in the pan, being sure to get the sides and all around.) If at any time the sauce becomes too thick, just whisk in a little more milk. If it's too thin, let it cook, stirring constantly, until it thickens again. It's that simple.

Add other ingredients according to the type of sauce you wish, and serve. Enjoy!

BROWN SAUCE

Cook the flour until it turns dark brown (do not burn), and prepare as for Off-White Sauce, using vegetable stock in place of the milk. Stir in 1 tablespoon tamari or 1 teaspoon dark miso (do not boil).

MUSHROOM SAUCE

Add 1 cup sautéed mushrooms (button, shiitake, portobello, etc.) to the sauce.

CHEESE SAUCE

Add ½ to 1 cup grated cheese to the finished Off-White Sauce. Try mozzarella, provolone, cheddar, Swiss (for a mornay sauce), Monterey Jack, farmer's, feta, soy mozzarella, or jalapeño soy cheese. Cook slowly just until the cheese melts.

BÉCHAMEL

Cut a peeled onion into quarters. Attach a whole bay leaf to ¼ of the onion with a tooth pick. Place the ¼ onion with the bay leaf into the sauce, and let it cook about 10 minutes. Remove. Adjust for thickness, if needed, and add a pinch of white pepper and a pinch of nutmeg.

Per ¼ cup: Calories 56, Protein 2 g, Fat 4 g, Carbohydrates 2 g

Miso Gravy

Yield: about 2 cups

As a child I loved "gravy-bread." While it was not at all difficult for me to give up meat, I really missed my "gravy-bread." Now I enjoy it whenever I like. Try this over mashed potatoes or with biscuits for a great breakfast.

Prepare as for the Brown Sauce recipe on page 86, being careful not to boil the miso. (That destroys much of the beneficial enzymes.) Enjoy!

ONION GRAVY

Sauté 2 tablespoons minced onion in the oil before adding the flour.

MUSHROOM GRAVY

Sauté 2 tablespoons sliced or chopped mushrooms in the oil before adding the flour. (Shiitakes are especially nice.)

MILK GRAVY

Use skim milk, soymilk, or rice milk in place of the vegetable stock.

2 tablespoons toasted sesame oil
2 tablespoons whole wheat pastry flour
2 cups dark vegetable stock
2 teaspoons dark miso
1 teaspoon mild molasses (optional)
Pinch of black pepper
Pinch of sage
Salt-free vegetable seasoning, to taste

VEGETARIAN "BACON" GRAVY

Add crumbled tempeh "bacon" (from T.L.T., page 113) to the miso gravy or milk gravy.

Per ¼ cup: Calories 43, Protein 1 g, Fat 2 g, Carbohydrates 2 g

Onion Sauce

Yield: 1¾ cups

Sauté the onion in the olive oil until translucent. In a small bowl, whisk together the arrowroot with ½ cup of the milk until smooth and there are no lumps. Add to the onions and reduce the heat to medium-low. Cook, stirring frequently with a wire whisk, until the mixture thickens. Add the seasonings, to taste. If the sauce gets too thick, add some more milk and stir. Serve over burgers or potatoes as you would gravy. Enjoy!

1 medium onion, minced
1 teaspoon extra-virgin olive oil
½ cup arrowroot
About ¾ cup soymilk or rice milk
1 teaspoon tamari
Pinch of sage or poultry seasoning
Pinch of black pepper
Salt-free vegetable seasoning, to taste

Per ¼ cup: Calories 56, Protein 1 g, Fat 1 g, Carbohydrates 10 g

Corn Salsa

Yield: about 2½ cups

Try this tasty variation of salsa verde at your next party or gathering for something uniquely different.

1 cup cooked corn
3 scallions, finely chopped
1 green or red bell pepper, diced
1 small can chopped mild chiles or the equivalent in fresh chiles
Jalapeño or other hot chiles, to taste
Juice of 2 limes
½ teaspoon chili powder (optional)
¼ cup minced fresh cilantro

Mix all the ingredients together, and refrigerate an hour or longer. Serve with chips or as a condiment. Enjoy!

VARIATIONS

Add chopped tomatoes, sun-dried tomatoes, cooked black, red, or pinto beans, minced garlic, or finely diced zucchini.

Per ¼ cup: Calories 21, Protein 0 g, Fat 0 g, Carbohydrates 5 g

Fresh Watermelon Salsa

Yield: about 2 cups

This salsa might sound strange, but try it with grilled tofu or veggies. It's quite good.

2 cups seeded, chopped watermelon
2 tablespoons minced red onion
2 tablespoons diced jicama
1 to 2 tablespoons mild chiles, roasted, peeled, and minced
1 to 2 cloves garlic, minced
1 teaspoon balsamic vinegar

Combine all the ingredients and mix together well. Refrigerate one hour or longer so the flavors will mingle. Serve and enjoy!

Per ¼ cup: Calories 16, Protein 0 g, Fat 0 g, Carbohydrates 3 g

Kiwi-Lime Salsa

Yield: about 2 cups

This is a tasty and unusual salsa. Try it on grilled tofu or seitan or as a colorful garnish with quesadillas.

Mix all the ingredients together well, and chill for an hour or longer to let the flavors mingle. Serve and enjoy!

4 to 6 kiwis, peeled and chopped
2 scallions, chopped
¼ cup minced red onion
1 yellow or red bell pepper, diced
Juice of 2 limes
¼ cup minced fresh cilantro
Jalapeños or other chiles, roasted, peeled, and minced, to taste

Per ¼ cup: Calories 42, Protein 1 g, Fat 0 g, Carbohydrates 9 g

Pineapple Salsa

Yield: 3 to 4 cups

Great with tofu or with Caribbean black bean enchiladas. For an impressive presentation, serve it in a pineapple shell.

1 small pineapple, cubed (about 2 cups)
1 small red onion, chopped
1 red bell pepper, diced
1 yellow bell pepper, diced
1 green bell pepper, diced
Fresh chiles, roasted, peeled, and minced, to taste
½ cup chopped fresh cilantro or mint
3 to 4 tablespoons lime juice

Combine all the ingredients in a mixing bowl, and toss well. Adjust the seasoning to taste. Serve immediately and enjoy!

VARIATIONS

Add 1 teaspoon balsamic vinegar to bring out more sweetness and flavor.

Toss a cup or so of cooked black or tepary beans with the rest of the ingredients, and serve over grilled tofu or seitan.

Per ¼ cup: Calories 30, Protein 0 g, Fat 0 g, Carbohydrates 7 g

Salsa de Barbacoa

Yield: 3 to 4 cups

While this sauce may not be quite traditional to the Southwest, it is delicious. Try it with beans as well as tofu, tempeh, or seitan.

1 medium onion, minced
1 teaspoon extra-virgin olive oil
2 to 4 cloves garlic, minced
2 cups tomato purée
1 tablespoon raw honey or brown
   rice syrup
1 tablespoon sorghum or
   unsulfured molasses
1 bottle beer (optional)
1 teaspoon dry mustard
Pinch of cayenne
Pinch of cloves
1 tablespoon chili powder
Juice of 2 lemons, or 2 tablespoons
   cider vinegar
1 tablespoon tamari
Salt-free vegetable seasoning, to
   taste

Sauté the onion in the oil in a heavy pan or skillet over medium heat until tender. Add the garlic and sauté another 2 to 3 minutes. Add the remaining ingredients and simmer for 20 to 30 minutes for optimum flavor. Enjoy!

VARIATIONS

Substitute the juice of 4 limes or 1 orange for the lemon juice. Remove the sauce from the heat after cooking, and add 1 tablespoon dark miso.

Mild or hot chiles, minced cilantro, chopped scallions or shallots, chopped sun-dried tomatoes, or sautéed, chopped mushrooms all add interest and flavor.

Per ¼ cup: Calories 34, Protein 1 g, Fat 0 g, Carbohydrates 7 g

Salsa Picante

Yield: 7 to 8 cups

It seems no Southwestern meal is complete without salsa picante. It can be frozen but will keep for quite a while in the refrigerator. This version is quite mild, but can easily be augmented with hotter chiles. I generally make two varieties of salsa—"wimpy" salsa and "4-alarm"—and let my family and friends choose for themselves according to how brave they feel.

Mix everything together in a large bowl, and refrigerate until ready to use. Serve with tortilla chips or as a condiment with most any food. Enjoy!

VARIATION

Add hotter chiles, especially a combination of varieties, to taste. Tabasco sauce, cayenne pepper, etc., also add a little kick to your salsa.

1 onion, diced
6 to 8 tomatoes, chopped
2 to 3 tomatillos, chopped (optional)
2 to 3 cloves garlic, minced
1 teaspoon chili powder
1 teaspoon cumin powder
1 tablespoon finely minced fresh cilantro
Juice of 1 lemon
Juice of 1 lime
1 avocado, chopped (optional)
1 to 2 mild fresh chiles, roasted, peeled, and minced

Per ¼ cup: Calories 14, Protein 0 g, Fat 0 g, Carbohydrates 3 g

Salsa Verde

Yield: 2 cups

Salsa verde (green salsa) is made with tomatillos, a small green fruit with a papery husk that resembles a green tomato. The tomatillos give the salsa a unique, slightly sweet flavor that goes especially well with New Mexican cuisine.

6 to 8 tomatillos, husks removed
  and chopped
½ small red onion, diced
2 roasted, peeled, and diced chilies,
  (or to taste)
2 to 3 cloves garlic, minced
Juice of 1 lime
¼ cup minced fresh cilantro

In a medium bowl, mix all the ingredients together well and refrigerate for an hour or longer to let the flavors marry. Use as you would tomato salsa on your favorite Southwestern dishes. Enjoy!

Per ¼ cup: Calories 25, Protein 1 g, Fat 0 g, Carbohydrates 5 g

Dill Sauce

Yield: 1 cup

This one's low-fat and works well for dipping raw vegetables also.

1 cup plain low-fat soy or dairy
  yogurt
1 tablespoon red wine vinegar
1 to 2 cloves minced garlic
  (optional)
1 teaspoon dill weed
1 teaspoon tamari
1 teaspoon honey or granulated
  sweetener (optional)

Whisk all the ingredients together well. Serve and enjoy!

Per 2 tablespoons: Calories 29, Protein 2 g, Fat 1 g, Carbohydrates 2 g

Corn Relish

Yield: about 5 cups

This colorful relish is a wonderful addition to a cookout or a picnic.

Mix everything together well and refrigerate several hours or overnight. Serve and enjoy!

VARIATIONS

Chopped red onion, cucumbers, or tomato make nice additions.

Substitute other salad dressings, such as honey-mustard for instance.

4 ears fresh corn, cut from the cob
1 green sweet bell pepper, diced
1 red sweet bell pepper, diced
1 cup Balsamic Vinaigrette, p. 82
¼ cup chopped fresh parsley or cilantro

Per serving: Calories 114, Protein 3 g, Fat 0 g, Carbohydrates 25 g

Garlic and Olive Oil

Yield: ½ cup

This is NOT a low-fat dip, but it is delicious. Enjoy it for special occasions, especially with steamed artichokes.

Whisk all the ingredients together well. Serve and enjoy!

½ cup extra-virgin olive oil
3 to 4 cloves garlic, minced
1 tablespoon finely minced fresh basil (optional)
¼ cup dairy or soy Parmesan (optional)

Per tablespoon: Calories 121, Protein 0 g, Fat 13 g, Carbohydrates 0 g

Guacamole

Yield: about 3 cups

This is a traditional favorite Southwestern food. Avocados are very high in fat and calories but are also extremely rich in vitamins, minerals, and enzymes. You might also substitute other green vegetables for all or part of the avocado (see variations).

1 avocado, peeled and chopped
1 tomatillo, green tomato, or red tomato, chopped
¼ cup chopped onion
1 tablespoon Salsa Picante, p. 91
1 teaspoon chili powder
Juice of 1 lime or lemon
1 teaspoon finely minced fresh cilantro

Mix everything together well, mashing it a little as you do. Serve with chips or as a condiment with burritos, enchiladas, etc. Enjoy!

VARIATIONS

To cut back the calories and fat, substitute all or part of the avocado with steamed spinach, asparagus, green beans, or peas. Mash very well or put through a food processor.

Per ¼ cup: Calories 34, Protein 0 g, Fat 1 g, Carbohydrates 3 g

Spicy Tomato Catch-up

Yield: about 2 cups

Commercial bottled ketchup (or catsup) is very high in sodium and is usually over 50% sugar! Here's a more healthful and tasty alternative. This freezes well also, so make plenty and keep it on hand.

In a medium mixing bowl, whisk together everything except the water until well blended. Add the water, a little at a time, until you have a fairly thick ketchup. Serve with oven-baked Ranch Fries, page 151, or bean burgers, pages 106-08. Enjoy!

1 cup tomato paste
¼ cup apple cider vinegar
¼ cup apple juice concentrate
1 tablespoon molasses
1 teaspoon onion powder
1 teaspoon garlic powder
1 teaspoon chili powder
1 teaspoon cumin
1 tablespoon tamari
Juice of 1 orange (optional)
Pinch of cloves
Salt-free vegetable seasoning, to taste
Pinch of cayenne (optional)
Approximately 2 tablespoons water

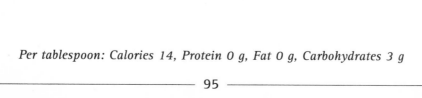

Per tablespoon: Calories 14, Protein 0 g, Fat 0 g, Carbohydrates 3 g

Tofu Mayonnaise

Yield: 2 cups

Regular mayonnaise are almost pure oil and egg yolk. One cup of mayo is about 1,600 calories! And, even worse, only about 5 of those calories are not from fat! This delicious, rich-tasting mayonnaise has about 90% fewer calories than regular mayonnaise. Almost everyone who has tasted it prefers it to regular mayonnaise. Generally, it will last about three weeks in the refrigerator, depending on the freshness of the tofu.

1 cup crumbled firm or extra-firm silken tofu

2 tablespoons prepared mustard (Dijon works well)

¼ cup lemon juice or mild vinegar

2 teaspoons tamari

2 teaspoons raw honey, brown rice syrup, or apple juice concentrate

¼ cup cold-pressed canola oil

In a blender, combine everything except the oil, and blend well. With the blender motor running, slowly pour in the oil, and blend until smooth. Adjust the flavors to taste. Refrigerate until ready to use. Enjoy!

VARIATIONS

Try a flavored vinegar—raspberry, balsamic, etc.—to give a different flavor.

Substitute olive, safflower (if you're not going to cook with the mayo), or toasted sesame oil for the canola oil.

Per tablespoon: Calories 24, Protein 1 g, Fat 2 g, Carbohydrates 0 g

Tofu Sour Cream

Yield: about 2 cups

Here's a delightful non-dairy (and lower fat) version of sour cream. Add chopped onions, garlic, or herbs, and use it as a dip for raw veggies, or serve it over a baked potato.

1½ cups crumbled firm tofu

¼ cup cold-pressed canola oil (optional)

¼ cup lemon juice

1 teaspoon tamari (optional)

Blend all the ingredients until smooth in a blender. Store in the refrigerator for up to a week. Enjoy!

LIME "SOUR CREAM"

Substitute lime juice for the lemon juice. Increase the amount of juice if you want a more pronounced flavor.

Per tablespoon: Calories 9, Protein 1 g, Fat 0 g, Carbohydrates 0 g

BReaDS aND SaNDWICHeS

YEAST BREADS

Yield: 2 loaves

No aroma stimulates the appetite with so much excitement, no texture and flavor satisfies the palate so completely as fresh baked bread. With modern technology, bread making can now be as simple as putting the ingredients into a machine and flipping a switch. Anyone baked bread in the supermarket or bakery. However, as tasty and convenient as these breads may be, there always seems to be one ingredient missing—love. When you mix and knead bread by hand, there's just no way possible to omit this "essential nutrient." The very decision to "go to that much trouble" implies you love someone enough to put that much of yourself into what you're doing. Of course, with today's busy schedules and the amount of time it takes to bake real bread, there are times when it just may be logistically impossible. However, when you do have a little time, or when it can be important enough to make the time, it's almost as easy to bake a couple of extra loaves and freeze them for use on those busy days when we can use a little of the extra love and nurturing that comes from home-baked bread. The actual working time is usually less than ½ hour; the rest of the time the bread is doing the work. Make bread on a day when you have other things to do at home. At other times, muffins, quickbreads, and so on can fill that role. Even if you've never baked a loaf of bread in your life, give it a try. It takes just a little practice, but the results are well worth the effort, and the more often you do it the easier it gets.
This is the perfect bread for beginners to practice with and for experts to enjoy. Don't be afraid to try some of the variations also.

2½ cups warm water
1 tablespoon raw honey
1 tablespoon active dry yeast
6 cups whole wheat flour*
¼ teaspoon sea salt (optional)

*If you substitute about one-fourth of the flour with vital wheat gluten, you will get a lighter loaf of bread.

Pick a spot in your kitchen to work that is draft-free. If possible, choose a counter or table that is not too low—your back will appreciate it. The best height is one that allows your arms to be fully extended with your palms resting on the table or counter.

Be sure your yeast is fresh. (It's usually dated for freshness when you buy it.) Mix the yeast with the warm water (105°F to 120°F, about baby bottle temperature). If the water is not hot enough, the yeast will not become activated, too hot and the yeast will die. Stir well to dissolve.

Stir in the honey until smooth. Set this aside and check it after about 10 to 15 minutes. If it's beginning to bubble or foam, the yeast is still active or good; if not, the yeast has died. Throw it away, buy some fresh yeast, and start over. This process of testing the yeast is called proofing.

Carefully stir in the salt and the flour, about 1 cup at a time. Stir and mix after every addition until the dough is smooth, elastic, and stiff—about 5 minutes. You'll get a feel for the texture and consistency of the dough with a little practice.

Turn the dough onto a well-floured board or counter. Rub a little flour on your hands, and start kneading. This is an essential step in bread making, because the kneading causes the gluten in the flour to become more elastic, so it will trap the bubbles of gas coming from the yeast. As these gas bubbles rise, they push up toward the surface, giving your bread a light, airy texture. Kneading takes a little practice, so please, don't be discouraged if your first few loaves are like adobe bricks. Just try again; you'll get it.

To knead, begin by folding the dough in half. Push down on the middle of the ball of dough with the heel of your hand, pushing the dough down and away from you. Be very aggressive with the dough. It greatly improves the elasticity of the dough and is great exercise for those arm muscles. Put some music on and think of it as kitchen exercises. Turn the ball of dough a quarter of a turn, fold it in half, and knead it again. If the dough becomes too sticky, sprinkle it with a bit of flour; if it becomes too dry, knead it some more. If it is still too dry and stiff, sprinkle the dough with a few drops of water.

Put a little oil into a large mixing bowl, and roll the ball of dough in the oil to cover it well. This prevents the dough from sticking to the bowl as it rises. Cover the bowl with a clean cloth or towel, and set it in a warm, draft-free spot. If you live in Arizona, that should be no problem; if you live in a cold climate and have a gas oven, simply place the bread in the oven with just the pilot light on. This will generate enough heat for the dough to rise. You can also place the dough on top of the refrigerator—hot air rises, so the top of the room is usually warmer than at counter level. If all else fails, preheat your oven to 350°F, turn it off, and place your ball of dough in the oven. Whichever method you choose, let the dough rise until it doubles in size, about 1½ hours.

Remove the dough from the bowl, and punch it down or knead it again for another minute or two. Divide the dough if it is to make more than one loaf. Shape into loaves. Put into oiled bread pans, and let it rise again until doubled in size, about 45 minutes.

Bake about 40 minutes at 375°F, or until the bread is golden brown and hollow sounding when tapped on the sides and bottom after it is removed from the pan. Enjoy!

Notes:

Salt helps with the leavening action to keep the rising under control, but, with a little practice, you can omit it if you like. I generally do not add salt to my bread dough.

Make a couple of loaves of dough, but before you shape it to rise in the pan, freeze the second one. When you're ready to bake it, place it in an oiled bread pan in a warm, draft-free spot to rise. (This may take about 4 hours.) Then bake as you would for fresh dough.

ONION-DILL BREAD

Add ½ cup minced onion and 2 teaspoons dill weed to the dough before kneading.

HERB BREAD

Add a handful of chopped herbs—dill, thyme, parsley, basil, rosemary, etc.—to the dough.

JALAPEÑO BREAD

Add about ¼ to ½ cup finely chopped jalapeños to the dough.

CINNAMON-RAISIN BREAD

Add ¼ cup ground cinnamon and ½ cup raisins to the dough.

NUT BREAD

Add 1 cup chopped nuts or seeds—walnuts, pecans, peanuts, sunflower seeds, etc. Also, try forming rolls or round loaves. Brush the top of the loaf with a little oil, and bake on a baking sheet.

Per slice (8 in a loaf): Calories 156, Protein 6 g, Fat 0 g, Carbohydrates 31 g

Love Buns

Yield: 12 buns

These wonderful rolls were discovered by my good friend, Jill Zuckerman, "The Amazing Jill."

In a small bowl, combine the warm water, yeast, and honey. Set aside in a warm place to proof (pages 98, 99).

Meanwhile, in a large bowl, combine the boiling water, oil, and sesame seeds. Stir in about 2 cups of the flour. When this sponge is lukewarm, add the yeast mixture (which should be active and bubbly).

Mix well and add the remaining flour, ½ cup at a time, until the dough is too stiff to stir. Turn the dough onto a floured surface, and knead until satiny smooth. Pinch off rolls of about 2 inches in diameter, and place into an oiled 9 x 14-inch baking dish, ½ inch apart. Let the dough rise for 30 minutes.

Bake for 25 minutes at 350°F.

½ cup warm water
1 tablespoon active dry yeast
1 teaspoon raw honey
1 cup boiling water
2 tablespoons cold-pressed canola oil
⅓ cup sesame seeds
3½ cups whole wheat flour
1 heart full of love

Per bun: Calories 161, Protein 5 g, Fat 5 g, Carbohydrates 24 g

Homemade Tortillas

Yield: About ten 8-inch tortillas

This is not authentic but it makes a simple, tasty tortilla that anyone can prepare and enjoy!

1 cup whole wheat pastry flour
1 cup yellow or blue cornmeal
5 tablespoons canola oil

Mix the flours together and add the oil. Mix in enough water to form a soft ball of dough. Pinch off a ball of dough slightly smaller than a golf ball, and press it between the palms of your hands to flatten slightly. Use a tortilla press or roll thinly on a piece of wax paper to form a flat, circular bread.

Heat a dry, heavy skillet over medium-high heat. When the skillet is hot, place the tortilla in the middle, and cook it until it bubbles and browns slightly on the bottom. Turn and cook the other side until it, too, begins to bubble. Remove the tortilla from the skillet, and serve. Enjoy!

Note: To keep the tortillas warm between the time you cook them and the time you serve them, preheat the oven to 350°F, and turn off the oven. Wrap the tortillas in a well-dampened but not dripping wet kitchen towel, and place them in the oven. You can keep the tortillas in the oven to stay warm for up to 20 to 30 minutes.

Per tortilla: Calories 150, Protein 3 g, Fat 7 g, Carbohydrates 19 g

Roasted Corn and Chile Corn Bread

Yield: 6 servings

This takes a little more work than other corn breads but is well worth it.

Shuck the corn and brush lightly with olive oil. Grill over a wood fire or broil under the broiler, turning often, until well browned. (You may also cut the raw corn from the cob, and toast it lightly in an oiled cast-iron skillet.) Cut the roasted kernels from the cob. The easiest way to do this is to lay the ear of corn horizontally on the cutting board, and cut from one end of the cob to the other.

Preheat the oven to 350°F. Brush a 9-inch cast-iron skillet or baking pan with olive oil, and place it in the oven to preheat.

In a large bowl, mix the dry ingredients, and blend well. Add the bell pepper, chiles, cilantro, and scallions, and stir into the dry ingredients.

In another bowl, mix together all the remaining oil, egg replacer, honey or maple syrup, milk, and lime juice. Add to the dry ingredients, and gently stir with a wooden spoon until just moistened. Do not beat or over mix, or the corn bread will be tough. If the batter is too dry, add more milk. Spoon into the hot skillet or baking pan.

Bake for 35 to 40 minutes, or until golden brown and a toothpick inserted in the center comes out dry and clean. Loosen the edges with a knife, and invert the pan onto a serving platter. Cut into squares and serve with butter or honey. Enjoy!

VARIATIONS

Hydrate and chop ¼ cup sun-dried tomatoes, and add to the batter.

Add a pinch of chili powder or oregano.

2 ears fresh corn on the cob*
3 tablespoons extra-virgin olive oil

Dry ingredients:
1¼ cups whole wheat pastry flour
¾ cup yellow or blue cornmeal
1 tablespoon baking powder
¼ teaspoon baking soda

½ cup mixed, chopped bell peppers (any color combination)
Fresh hot chiles (anaheim, jalapeños, serranos, or habaneros), roasted, peeled, and minced, to taste
¼ cup finely chopped fresh cilantro or parsley
2 scallions, finely chopped

Wet ingredients:
Egg replacer equivalent to 2 eggs, p. 24
3 tablespoons raw honey or maple syrup
1 cup skim milk, soymilk, or rice milk
Juice of 1 lime

*If you don't have time to grill the corn, use canned or frozen whole kernels (organic, of course).

Per serving: Calories 290, Protein 8 g, Fat 8 g, Carbohydrates 45 g

Squash Bread

Yield: 2 loaves

You say you can't get your children to eat vegetables? Serve them this sweet, spicy bread—just don't tell them what's in it. They'll gobble it up and ask for more!

½ cup cold-pressed canola oil

Egg replacer equivalent to 3 eggs, p. 24

¾ cup raw honey or granulated sweetener

1 tablespoon pure vanilla extract

2 cups grated zucchini, yellow crookneck, or other squash

3 cups whole wheat pastry flour

1 teaspoon non-aluminum baking powder

1 teaspoon cinnamon

½ teaspoon baking soda

Preheat the oven to 325°F.

In a large mixing bowl, combine the oil, egg replacer, honey, vanilla, and squash. In another bowl, stir together the dry ingredients, mixing well. Pour the wet ingredients into the dry ingredients, and mix well but don't beat. Pour into 2 oiled loaf pans. Bake about 1 hour or until a toothpick inserted in the center comes out clean. Try this bread toasted also. Enjoy!

VARIATIONS

Substitute cooked pumpkin or sweet potatoes for the squash, add 2 more tablespoons flour, and a pinch of cloves, mace, and allspice.

Add 1 cup chopped walnuts, pecans, sunflower seeds, or raisins.

Per slice (8 per loaf): Calories 194, Protein 4 g, Fat 7 g, Carbohydrates 28 g

Whole Wheat Biscuits

Yield: 6 to 8 servings

These are very simple, either as rolled or drop biscuits. They are especially tasty with vegetarian gravy.

Preheat the oven to 450°F.

Stir the dry ingredients together with a fork. Make a well in the center Roll the dough ¼ to ½ inch thick, and cut with a 2-inch round cutter. (A small juice glass or a tin can with both ends removed will work very well.) Dip the edge of the cutter in flour to prevent sticking. Place the biscuits touching each other on a baking sheet. (You don't need to oil the sheet, but if you do, they'll get nice and crusty.) Bake for 10 to 15 minutes, or until the biscuits are golden brown. Check the bottoms to be sure they don't burn. Serve hot with honey, jam, or gravy. Enjoy!

3 cups whole wheat pastry flour

2 teaspoons non-aluminum baking powder

1½ cups skim milk, rice milk, or soymilk

2 tablespoons cold-pressed canola oil

VARIATIONS

Substitute all or part of the whole wheat flour with other varieties—barley, oat, rice, buckwheat flour, etc.

Use buttermilk, soured milk, or soymilk. To make soured milk, simply add 1 teaspoon lemon juice or vinegar to 1 cup of milk or soymilk, and let the mixture set for a few minutes to sour. If using soured milk in this recipe, cut the baking powder to 1 teaspoon, and add ½ teaspoon baking soda.

SOURDOUGH BISCUITS

Substitute ½ cup sourdough starter for ½ cup of the flour and some of the milk. Let the dough set overnight, as for Sourdough Pancakes, page 43. The next morning, add ½ teaspoon baking soda and the oil. Prepare as for Whole Wheat Biscuits.of the dry ingredients, and add the liquid ingredients. Stir just enough to moisten, then turn the dough onto a well-floured board, and knead a little.

The heart of his breakfast was a plenitude of sourdough biscuits, which he cooked in a Dutch oven out in the backyard.

—Larry McMurtry

Per biscuit: Calories 228, Protein 8 g, Fat 6 g, Carbohydrates 37 g

Black Bean Patties

Yield: 6 patties

Top with your favorite salsa, and serve with warm tortillas and a salad for a simple, light meal. Or serve as a burger with lettuce, tomatoes, and avocado.

3 cups cooked, drained black beans
1 red onion, chopped
1 red or green bell pepper, diced
2 chiles, roasted, peeled, and
    minced
½ cup frozen or fresh corn
    (optional)
2 to 3 cloves garlic, minced
1 tablespoon chili powder
½ teaspoon ground cumin
1 tablespoon tomato paste
¼ cup minced fresh cilantro
1 cup cornmeal
Olive or canola oil for pan frying
    (optional)

These may be baked or pan fried. If baking, preheat the oven to 375°F.

Using a potato masher or heavy fork, mash the beans into a thick paste. Combine with the rest of the ingredients, except the cornmeal. Mix together well and form into burger patties. Dredge the patties in the cornmeal, and pan fry until well browned on each side, or place on an oiled baking sheet, and bake about 15 minutes per side. Serve hot and enjoy!

VARIATIONS

Substitute other varieties of beans.

Add sun-dried tomatoes, chopped olives, or mushrooms to the mixture.

Per patty: Calories 219, Protein 9 g, Fat 0 g, Carbohydrates 43 g

Lentil-Nut Burger

Yield: 4 burgers

This will surprise—and satisfy—many a "meat 'n' potatoes" fan. This burger is low-fat and quite delicious; top it with a slice of soy or dairy cheese for a "cheese burger."

Preheat the oven to 375°F.

Mix all the ingredients together in a medium bowl, and mash with a fork or potato masher until the mixture is fairly smooth and will hold together. Form 4 burger patties, place on a lightly oiled baking sheet, and bake 25 minutes. Carefully turn the burgers over, and top each with 2 tablespoons of the barbecue sauce and a slice of cheese, if desired. Bake 10 minutes more.

Serve hot on a whole-grain roll with your favorite burger fixings. Enjoy!

VARIATIONS

Substitute cooked brown rice for the bulgur or rolled wheat for the oats.

Almost any bean will substitute well for the lentils.

1 cup cooked, drained lentils
1 tablespoon miso
1 tablespoon tahini
1 tablespoon finely minced onion
1 to 2 cloves garlic, minced
½ cup cooked bulgur
½ cup chopped nuts
Salt-free vegetable seasoning, to taste
Salsa de Barbacoa, p. 90, or your favorite barbeque sauce
Cheese slices (optional)

Per burger: Calories 213, Protein 8 g, Fat 10 g, Carbohydrates 21 g

Shiitake Oatburger

Yield: 6 burgers

Tasty and simple, this quick burger recipe will delight kids and grown-ups alike. Try some of the variations for a change of pace.

½ small onion, minced
½ cup chopped shiitake
    mushrooms
2 cloves garlic, minced
1 teaspoon tamari and 1 teaspoon
    water
1¼ cups rolled oats
½ cup cooked, drained pinto beans
1 teaspoon dry basil,
    or 1 tablespoon fresh basil
¼ cup barbecue sauce
½ cup grated dairy or soy cheese
½ cup cornmeal
Olive or canola oil for frying

In a medium skillet, braise the onion, mushrooms, and garlic in the tamari and water until soft. In a large mixing bowl, mash the beans with a potato masher, add the rest of the ingredients (except the cornmeal), and mix together well, using your hands to really get in there and mix it together. Let the mixture rest for about 10 minutes so the oats will soften and absorb moisture.

Form into six burgers and dredge in the cornmeal. Either fry in a little olive oil until hot throughout and crispy on the outside, or bake on an oiled baking sheet in a preheated 400°F oven, cooking 10 minutes on a side. Serve with Onion Sauce, page 87, or on a whole-grain roll with your favorite burger trimmings. Enjoy!

VARIATIONS

Chop other vegetables—zucchini, button mushrooms, etc.—and use in place of the shiitake mushrooms.

Substitute other beans or seasonings.

Try cooked rice or other grains in place of rolled oats.

Try other rolled grains—quinoa, kamut, etc.

Per burger: Calories 195, Protein 8 g, Fat 4 g, Carbohydrates 31 g

Open-Faced Broccoli with Cheese Sauce

Yield: 6 servings

This is a great way to get kids to eat their vegetables. It's very versatile and can be changed to please almost anyone. Perhaps even George Bush?

Seer the mushrooms over low heat in a dry pan, stirring often. If they start to stick, add 1 tablespoon water, stock, or wine.

Mix the arrowroot with the milk in a medium saucepan, and heat slowly. Mix in the cheese and stir until thick and smooth. If it gets too thick, add a little more milk to thin.

Layer the sandwich by placing 2 split biscuit halves or a split English muffin half on the bottom, then sliced tomatoes, broccoli, sautéed mushrooms, and a topping of cheese sauce. Serve hot and enjoy!

VARIATIONS

Try most any vegetable. I've made this with cauliflower, asparagus, and green beans. They're all great.

Try other breads, toasted.

A slice of onion on the tomato is nice.

Sprinkle a few chopped nuts or sunflower seeds (toasted or raw) on top.

A slice of tofu, plain, marinated, or cooked makes a nice addition.

For a more Southwestern flavor, add some chopped chiles or use a pepper Jack cheese.

½ pound mushrooms, sliced
2 tablespoons arrowroot or cornstarch
½ cup skim milk or soymilk
½ pound white cheddar, Swiss, mozzarella, or soy mozzarella, grated
12 Whole Wheat Biscuits, p. 105, or 6 English muffins
2 tomatoes, sliced
3 cups chopped broccoli, steamed

Per serving: Calories 340, Protein 17 g, Fat 13 g, Carbohydrates 36 g

Open-Faced Seitan-Pepper Sandwich with Hot Onion Gravy

Yield: 4 servings

Seitan is a wonderful product made from wheat gluten. It's available in health food stores and Oriental markets. With its beefy texture, seitan will satisfy all of your wranglers around the campfire.

1 (16-ounce) package marinated seitan
1 teaspoon toasted sesame oil
½ cup diced onions
½ cup julienned red bell peppers
½ cup julienned green bell peppers
1 cup sliced shiitake mushrooms

Gravy:
1 teaspoon tamari
2 teaspoons arrowroot or cornstarch

2 sourdough whole wheat rolls, cut in half

Drain the seitan, but reserve the liquid to make the gravy. Thinly slice the seitan. Heat a heavy skillet over medium-high heat. Add the oil, onion, peppers, mushrooms, and seitan. Sauté quickly, stirring frequently until the vegetables are tender.

In another small skillet, mix the reserved seitan liquid with the tamari and arrowroot until the arrowroot is well dissolved. Cook slowly, stirring constantly, until thickened. Add to the seitan-vegetable mixture, and heat through. Pour over the rolls and serve. Enjoy!

VARIATIONS

Other vegetables, such as zucchini and garlic, work well, either with or instead of the ingredients in this sandwich.

Textured vegetable protein, tempeh, and tofu also substitute well for the seitan.

A pinch of miso, mixed in well at the end, adds a wonderful flavor.

Per serving: Calories 293, Protein 42 g, Fat 3 g, Carbohydrates 25 g

Sloppy Joses

Yield: 8 servings

As good or better than any Sloppy Joes you've ever tasted. Please don't let the amount of ingredients intimidate you; it's very simple. Serve with lots of napkins.

In a large, heavy skillet, sauté the onions, peppers, and tomatoes in the oil over low heat until tender. Add the garlic and sauté another 2 to 3 minutes. Add the rest of the ingredients, cover, and cook over medium-low heat about 20 to 30 minutes. Uncover and cook another 10 minutes, or until the mixture is thick and the flavors have all married well. Serve on whole-grain rolls with lettuce, tomato slices, and pickles or cucumber slices. Enjoy!

VARIATIONS

Substitute tempeh, tofu, or another variety of textured vegetable protein.

Shiitake mushrooms or diced zucchini are good additions. Add to the onions, peppers, and tomatoes.

A touch of orange juice may sound strange, but try adding it with or instead of lemon or lime juice.

Chopped fresh cilantro adds an exotic touch.

2 cups diced onions
1 cup diced red bell peppers
1 cup diced green bell peppers
3 cups chopped tomatoes
2 teaspoons extra-virgin olive oil
4 to 5 cloves garlic, minced
2 cups textured vegetable protein granules, hydrated in 1¾ cups boiling water
2 cups tomato purée
1½ tablespoons tamari
¼ cup lemon or lime juice
1 tablespoon chili powder
1 tablespoon cumin
2 teaspoons dry mustard
Pinch of cayenne
Pinch of cloves
Pinch of cinnamon
1 tablespoon sorghum or unsulfured molasses (optional)

Per serving: Calories 139, Protein 12 g, Fat 1 g, Carbohydrates 19 g

Southwestern Falafels

Yield: 6 to 8 servings

Falafels are small, deep-fried fritters made from puréed chick-peas (garbanzo beans). Baking, however, gives you all of the flavor of the traditional dish with much less fat. Alright, if you want to be a purist about it, they are traditionally a Middle Eastern dish, but with the right seasonings, they are delicious wrapped in a tortilla with salsa, chopped onions, and black olives. Be creative, break tradition!

3 cups cooked chick-peas
2 to 3 cloves garlic, minced
⅓ cup whole wheat cracker crumbs
Egg replacer equivalent to 1 egg,
    p. 24, or 2 egg whites
2 teaspoons chopped fresh cilantro
Pinch of cayenne or chili powder
    (optional)

Grind the chick-peas in a food processor or blender. Scrape into a bowl and add the remaining ingredients. Roll into about 1-inch balls. These may be made ahead and refrigerated until cooking time.

Preheat the oven to 400°F.

Place the balls on an oiled baking sheet, not quite touching. Bake about 20 to 25 minutes, or until golden brown and crispy.

VARIATIONS

Wheat germ may be used in place of the cracker crumbs.

To further mix the ethnicity, try serving in a pita pocket with lettuce, salsa, avocado, and grated cheese, like a Middle Eastern taco!

Per serving: Calories 141, Protein 7 g, Fat 2 g, Carbohydrates 23 g

Tempeh, Lettuce, and Tomato
T.L.T.

Yield: 4 servings

A good friend of mine, a real "meat and potatoes" guy, swore that he'd never buy bacon again after tasting this recipe. He likes the tempeh much better. This is not what you would call a low-calorie sandwich, but it's definitely lower than if it were made with bacon. It's also lower in fat, has no cholesterol, and an animal didn't have to die to make it. I like to pack a couple of these sandwiches before a day hiking in the Arizona desert.

To make the tempeh bacon, heat a heavy skillet over medium-high heat. Add about 2 tablespoons of the oil. Fry the tempeh slices until crispy. Add more oil as it becomes necessary, but always try to use as little as you can get by with. Turn and fry on the other side.

Remove from the heat and drain on paper towels. Sprinkle lightly with tamari and vegetable seasoning. Serve on the slices of toasted whole-grain bread with lettuce, tomato, and onion slices (optional). Spread the toast with mustard or Tofu Mayo. Enjoy!

Tempeh Bacon:
Approximately ⅓ cup toasted sesame oil
1 (8-ounce) package tempeh, thinly sliced (making about 25 slices)
2 tablespoons tamari
Salt-free vegetable seasoning, to taste

8 slices whole-grain toast
Lettuce, tomato, and onion slices for 4 sandwiches
Mustard or Tofu Mayo, p. 96

Per serving: Calories 297, Protein 15 g, Fat 12 g, Carbohydrates 30 g

Tempeh Salad Sandwich

Yield: 6 servings

Take this delicious sandwich along on a picnic, or enjoy with your friends while watching the big game on TV. Anyway you serve it, it's a great sandwich.

3 tablespoons Tofu Mayo, p. 96, or your favorite tofu mayonnaise

2 tablespoons spicy or Dijon mustard

1 tablespoon toasted sesame oil

1 tablespoon frozen apple juice concentrate

1 (8-ounce) package tempeh, cubed and steamed for 15 minutes

3 tablespoons minced red onion

½ cup minced celery

¼ cup diced jicama or cucumber

½ cup chopped apple or pear (optional)

¼ cup sunflower seeds

Salt-free vegetable seasoning, to taste

In a large bowl, mix together the mayo, mustard, oil, and juice concentrate.

Combine with the rest of the ingredients. Serve on a whole grain roll, rye toast, or pita pocket with lettuce, sprouts, and sliced tomato, or, perhaps, stuffed in a tomato. Enjoy!

Note:

Frozen apple juice concentrate can be kept defrosted in the refrigerator, usually for a month or longer. Use undiluted in this recipe.

VARIATIONS

Add a pinch of poultry seasoning for a more familiar taste.

Substitute blueberries for the apple or pear.

Diced red or green bell pepper adds a little color. Also try some frozen peas.

Some finely minced parsley, or even cilantro, might be nice.

Per salad serving: Calories 160, Protein 8 g, Fat 9 g, Carbohydrates 10 g

MAIN DISHES

The chile lover knows that pain can be transformed into a friendly sensation whose strength can go into making him high.

—Andrew Weil

Baja Beans and Franks
(Not-Dog Style)

Yield: 8 servings

A variation of Boston baked beans with a south-of-the-border flare. Kids of all ages love these. They're really not difficult to make, but they do take a while to cook. Use a crock-pot or slow-cooker. Leftovers are great rolled in a tortilla. They also freeze very well.

2 cups navy beans

1 onion, chopped
3 tomatoes, chopped
2 to 3 cloves garlic, minced
1 bell pepper, diced (optional)
2 tablespoons black-strap molasses
1 tablespoon pure maple syrup,
  raw honey, or brown rice syrup
1 tablespoon apple cider vinegar or
  lemon juice
1 teaspoon dry mustard
¼ cup mild chiles
1 teaspoon chili powder
Tamari or miso, to taste (optional)
8 meatless franks, cut into ½-inch
  pieces

Soak the beans overnight in enough water to cover. Drain the beans, cover with fresh water, and simmer for 1 hour, or until well cooked and tender.

Preheat the oven to 300°F.

Mix the beans with the rest of the ingredients, and place in a 2-quart casserole dish with a lid. Bake about 2 to 4 hours, stirring only a couple of times. Add a little water as needed, but don't drown them, please.

Or, if you prefer, mix everything together in a slow-cooker or crock-pot, and simmer for several hours or all day.

Serve hot with corn bread and a salad. Enjoy!

VARIATIONS

Chop 2 unpeeled apples or pears, and add to the mixture.

One (6-ounce) can of tomato paste or a handful of chopped rehydrated sun-dried tomatoes all add a very nice flavor.

Add the juice of 2 limes.

Add a little grated carrot and/or thinly sliced celery.

A pinch of cloves or cinnamon would add a nice subtle spiciness. Be careful not to over spice.

Per serving: Calories 277, Protein 17 g, Fat 3 g, Carbohydrates 45 g

Bean Burritos

Yield: 4 servings

The word burrito means "little burro," so these wrapped sandwiches are often called burros. As the story was told to me, Mexican children wrap the beans in the tortilla in such a way that it appears to have two long ears, like a burro. You'll call these great eating.

4 whole wheat tortillas
2 to 3 cups Frijoles, p. 150

Divide the beans up among the tortillas, placing then toward the middle but slightly more to one side. Fold the tortilla envelope-style around the beans (first one side, then both ends, and finally roll). Eat sandwich-style or, if preferred, top with a little grated dairy or soy cheese and salsa, and heat in a 350°F oven about 15 to 20 minutes. Serve with shredded lettuce, guacamole, Tofu Sour Cream, page 96, etc. Enjoy!

VARIATIONS

Rehydrated sun-dried tomatoes and sautéed mushrooms may be added to the beans and rolled in the tortilla.

Per serving: Calories 226, Protein 10 g, Fat 2 g, Carbohydrates 42 g

Black Beans and Baked Polenta with Lime "Sour Cream"

Yield: 6 servings

Although polenta is generally considered more of an Italian dish, it lends itself very well to Mexican or Southwest influences. Try it also topped with salsa, chili, frijoles, or other sauces and toppings. The polenta needs to cool thoroughly before slicing, but it can be made a day or two ahead of serving.

Polenta:
2½ cups yellow or blue cornmeal
2½ tablespoons extra-virgin olive oil

3 cups cooked black beans
1 cup salsa
1 cup grated soy or dairy cheese
¼ cup minced fresh cilantro
6 cherry tomatoes, for garnish (optional)
1½ cups Lime "Sour Cream," p. 96

To make the polenta, oil an 8 x 4-inch baking pan well with olive oil, and set aside.

Although it is not necessary, toasting the cornmeal first brings out flavor and makes it easier to digest. Simply heat a large, heavy skillet over medium heat, and lightly toast the cornmeal until it becomes aromatic, but not quite browned. Pour it into a bowl, and let it cool.

In a medium saucepan, bring 3 cups of cold water to a boil. While waiting for the water to boil, combine the cooled cornmeal with 2¾ cups cold water, and mix together well. Pour this mixture into the boiling water, stirring constantly to prevent sticking. When the mixture begins to boil, reduce the heat to low, and cover the pot. Cook the polenta about 45 to 50 minutes, or until it is very thick and soft and all the water is absorbed.

Stir 2 tablespoons of the oil into the mixture, and spoon it into the oiled baking pan, using your hand or a spoon that has been dipped in cold water to press the mixture into the pan. Rub the remaining oil over the top of the polenta, and let the polenta cool. Cover with waxed paper or

plastic wrap, and store in the refrigerator for up to 2 days.

Preheat the oven to 400°F.

Cut the cold polenta into 6 pieces, and place them on an oiled baking sheet.

Spread each piece with black beans, and top with salsa and grated cheese. Top each slice with a cherry tomato and a sprinkle of minced cilantro. Bake for 30 to 35 minutes, or until it's heated through and the cheese is melted and bubbly. Serve hot with a dollop of Lime "Sour Cream." Enjoy!

VARIATIONS

You might want to flavor the polenta by adding garlic, grated cheese, or spices and herbs—basil, cilantro, chili powder, cumin, etc.—to the mixture before cooling.

Per serving: Calories 460, Protein 19 g, Fat 10 g, Carbohydrates 71 g

Black Bean and Posole Burritos

Yield: 6 burritos

Posole is a Mexican version of hominy. If you can't find posole, substitute hominy instead. Serve with Spanish rice and calabacitas for a delicious repast.

2 cups cooked posole or hominy
2 cups cooked black beans
1 red onion, chopped
1 to 2 cloves garlic, minced
4 tomatoes, chopped,
    or 1 (28-ounce) can chopped
    tomatoes
Chiles, roasted, peeled, and minced,
    to taste
1 teaspoon chili powder
½ teaspoon cumin powder
¼ cup minced fresh cilantro
6 whole wheat tortillas

In a large, heavy skillet, combine all the ingredients, except the tortillas, and cook 30 minutes or longer until well-heated and slightly thick. Wrap burrito-style in a tortilla, and serve. Enjoy!

VARIATIONS

Substitute other beans or grains.

Add sautéed bell peppers, mushrooms, corn, or squash.

Per burrito: Calories 221, Protein 8 g, Fat 2 g, Carbohydrates 42 g

Black Bean and Seitan Burrito

Yield: 6 burritos

The seitan adds texture and the beans and corn combine for a wonderfully satisfying flavor. Salsa verde gives it a flavor reminiscent of Taos or Santa Fe.

In a large, heavy skillet, sauté the onion in the olive oil or stock until tender, stirring often. Add the bell pepper, tomatoes, zucchini or mushrooms, and garlic, and sauté another 5 minutes or so. Stir in the chili powder, chiles, about half of the cilantro, the lime juice, and balsamic vinegar, and cook until heated through.

Preheat the oven to 350°F, then turn the oven off. Wrap the tortillas in a clean, damp towel, and place in the hot oven for about 7 to 8 minutes, or until soft and heated through.

Layer ⅙ of the beans, seitan, corn, and vegetable mixture on each tortilla, and roll envelope-style (first fold one side over, fold both ends in, and roll the burro up). Serve hot garnished with the Salsa Verde, remaining cilantro, and crumbled feta cheese. Enjoy!

VARIATIONS

Substitute tofu, tempeh, or textured vegetable protein in place of the seitan.

Anasazi, pinto, adzuki, kidney, or tepary beans all work well in this.

Try other vegetables such as leeks, yellow squash, yams (delicious), shiitake mushrooms, etc. Garnish with pine nuts.

½ onion, chopped
1 tablespoon olive oil or vegetable stock
1 red or green bell pepper, diced
2 tomatoes, chopped
½ cup thinly sliced zucchini or mushrooms
2 to 3 cloves garlic, minced
1 tablespoon chili powder
Chiles, roasted, peeled, and minced, to taste
½ cup minced fresh cilantro
Juice of 1 lime
1 teaspoon balsamic vinegar
2 cups cooked black beans
2 cups thinly shredded seitan
2 ears of corn, cut from the cob, or 1 cup frozen corn
6 large whole wheat tortillas
1 cup Salsa Verde, p. 92
1 cup feta cheese (optional)

Per burrito: Calories 300, Protein 23 g, Fat 4 g, Carbohydrates 41 g

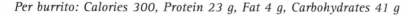

Black Bean and Sweet Potato Enchiladas

Yield: 4 servings

Quite different, but very tasty. Be sure to try some of the variations also.

1 yellow onion, chopped
Water, red wine, or vegetable stock
   for braising
2 to 3 cloves garlic, minced

2 medium sweet potatoes or yams,
   cooked and diced
1 cup cooked black beans
1 red or green bell pepper, diced
Jalapeños or other chiles, to taste
1 teaspoon cumin powder
1 teaspoon coriander
1 teaspoon chili powder
Pinch of cardamom (optional)
1 tablespoon minced fresh cilantro

8 corn tortillas
1 cup Salsa Verde, p. 92

Braise the onion in water or a little red wine or vegetable stock until tender. Add the garlic and braise another 5 minutes. Add everything but the tortillas and salsa, and cook over low heat until it thickens.

Preheat the oven to 350°F. Heat the tortillas lightly in a dry griddle to soften them so they don't tear when filling. Spoon a little of the filling onto the tortillas, and place seam side down on an oiled baking dish. Top with the salsa verde, and bake for about 10 minutes, or until heated through. Serve hot with Frijoles, page 150, and Spanish rice. Enjoy!

VARIATIONS

Try different beans—red, anasazi, tepary, adzuki, pinto, etc.

Try other vegetables, with or instead of the sweet potatoes—potatoes, shiitake or button mushrooms, greens, corn, diced carrots, etc.

Add a couple of tomatoes to the filling mix or use a tomato salsa.

Per serving: Calories 304, Protein 10 g, Fat 2 g, Carbohydrates 61 g

Black Beans and Rice

Moors and Christians
Frijoles Negros y Arroz
Blancos y Negros

Yield: 6 servings

One of the truly great ethnic dishes, this can also be done with red, kidney, or pinto beans, and it's wonderful with each. Serve with tortillas or spicy corn bread.

In a dry skillet over medium heat, sauté the onions and chiles about 5 minutes, or until the onion is tender. Add the garlic, lime juice, and seasonings, and cook another 2 to 3 minutes. Add the beans and cook another 5 to 10 minutes, or until well heated and the flavors are well married. Serve over the brown rice. Garnish with a dollop of Tofu Sour Cream, some chopped scallions, and cherry tomatoes cut to form flowers, page 77. Enjoy!

½ cup chopped onions
Mild or hot chiles, to taste
2 to 3 cloves garlic, minced
Juice of 1 lime or lemon
1 teaspoon chili powder
1 teaspoon cumin powder
2 teaspoons finely minced fresh cilantro
Salt-free vegetable seasoning, to taste

3 cups cooked black beans
2 cups cooked brown rice
Tofu Sour Cream, p. 96, for garnish
Chopped scallions or chives, for garnish
6 cherry tomatoes, for garnish

Per serving: Calories 196, Protein 8 g, Fat 0 g, Carbohydrates 39 g

Chiles Rellenos

Yield: 12 servings

This dish usually requires larger chile peppers, usually the milder chiles—Anaheim and poblanos, etc. Traditionally these are deep fried, but I have found they work very well being baked in the oven.

12 fresh, large mild chiles, roasted, peeled, and seeded
3 cups cheddar, Monterey Jack, or soy jalapeño cheese, grated or cut into long, thin sticks
1 cup whole wheat pastry flour
½ cup cornmeal
1 teaspoon chili powder
2 cups Enchilada Sauce, p. 125

Preheat the oven to 400°F.

Stuff the peppers with the grated cheese, being careful not to tear them. In a medium bowl, mix the flour, cornmeal, and chili powder, and add enough water to make a stiff batter.

Make sure that the outside of the pepper is dry so the batter will stick. Dip each pepper into the batter, and arrange it on an oiled baking sheet. Bake about 20 minutes or until golden brown. Top with the enchilada sauce, and bake another 10 minutes. Serve with shredded lettuce and guacamole. Enjoy!

VARIATIONS

For vegan chiles, stuff with 3 cups crumbled firm tofu sautéed with onion, garlic, and chili powder, to taste.

Try filling the chiles with beans or Frijoles, page 150.

For a lighter batter, add ½ teaspoon baking soda and substitute buttermilk, soured milk, or soymilk for the water.

Enlightenment embodies compassion. If you're using hot peppers in your dishes, please be merciful and at least inform your guests.

—Baba Bob

Per serving: Calories 196, Protein 10 g, Fat 9 g, Carbohydrates 17 g

Enchiladas con Queso

Yield: 6 servings

These are very satisfying and tasty—a great improvement over the fast-food variety.

Notice that the filling and the sauce contain almost the same ingredients. I generally put 2 pans on the stove and put a sticker in front of each with "filling" or "sauce" written on it so I don't become confused. Then I just go down the list putting ingredients in both. It's very simple.

In 2 saucepans, sauté the onions in the water or wine. Add the tomatoes, chiles, and seasonings. Cook until tender. Turn off the heat.

Add the cheese to the filling pan, and stir until the cheese melts.

For a smoother sauce, place ½ of the saucepan mixture in a blender, and blend. Add back to the rest of the sauce.

Divide the filling among the 6 tortillas. You can make the tortillas more pliable by heating them first. Simply wrap them in a damp towel, and place in a preheated 300°F oven for about 10 minutes.

Roll the tortillas up and place them seam-side down in an oiled baking dish. Cover with the enchilada sauce and, if desired, a little more cheese. Bake until hot and the cheese is well melted, about 5 to 10 minutes. Serve with shredded lettuce, salsa, guacamole, and Tofu Sour Cream, page 96. Enjoy!

VARIATIONS

Fill with Frijoles, page 150, or Calabacitas, page 143.

SPINACH AND WALNUT ENCHILADAS

Substitute 2 cups cooked, drained spinach and ½ cup chopped walnuts for the cheese in the filling.

6 corn or blue corn tortillas

Enchilada Filling:
½ cup chopped onions
¼ cup water or red wine
½ cup chopped tomatoes
¼ cup chopped mild or hot chiles
1 tablespoon chili powder
1 teaspoon cumin powder
2 cups grated dairy or soy cheese

Enchilada Sauce:
½ cup chopped onions
¼ cup water or red wine
½ cup chopped tomatoes
¼ cup chopped chiles
1 tablespoon chili powder
1 teaspoon cumin powder
1 teaspoon red wine vinegar
2 to 3 cloves garlic, minced

Per serving: Calories 172, Protein 11 g, Fat 11 g, Carbohydrates 5 g

Feijoada

Yield: 6 servings

Feijoada is a traditional dish of Brazil, but it fits in very well with Southwestern cuisine. No one has ever complained about its inclusion. Usually made from leftover meats, this light, vegetarian version makes use of tempeh, instead, but loses none of the tropical flavor.

12 ounces tempeh
1 tablespoon tamari
4 cloves garlic, minced

1 small onion, chopped
1 tablespoon extra-virgin olive oil
  or vegetable stock
3 cups cooked black beans
1 cup vegetable stock
2 bay leaves
1 teaspoon cumin powder
Juice of 1 orange
Juice of 2 limes
Cayenne or other chile, to taste

Crumble the tempeh into a bowl, and sprinkle with the tamari and garlic. Set aside to marinate.

In a heavy skillet over medium heat, sauté the onion in the olive oil or vegetable stock until tender. Add the tempeh and marinade, and sauté another 5 to 10 minutes. Add the remaining ingredients, and reduce the heat to a low simmer. Cook another 10 to 15 minutes to blend the flavors. Serve with rice and enjoy!

VARIATIONS

Mushrooms, zucchini or yellow squash, tomatoes, bell peppers, potatoes, or sweet potatoes would all add nutrition and flavor.

Minced cilantro, chives, or shallots would make a nice garnish and add more flavor.

Per serving: Calories 256, Protein 16 g, Fat 6 g, Carbohydrates 33 g

Over-Stuffed Peppers

Yield: 8 servings

Peppers can be stuffed with a myriad of delightful ingredients and flavors. Corn bread or muffins make a great accompaniment.

Preheat the oven to 350°F.

In a large, heavy skillet, heat the oil and sauté the onions, celery, carrot, and bell pepper until tender. Add the garlic and sauté another 2 to 3 minutes. Add the rice, beans, tahini, and seasonings. Mix well.

Stuff each pepper with the mixture. Place them in a baking dish with about ½ cup of water in the bottom of the dish to prevent the peppers from drying out. Bake 25 to 35 minutes, or until the peppers are soft. Serve hot with a dollop of salsa or guacamole, and enjoy!

Note: Green bell peppers are not ripe and may give some people indigestion. Red, yellow, and orange bell peppers are fully ripened. If you get indigestion from eating green peppers, try the ripe ones.

VARIATIONS

Substitute most any grain or combination of grains for the rice—millet, quinoa, amaranth, barley, wheat berries, wild rice, etc.

Substitute beans—lentils, pintos, kidney, anasazi, black, lima, etc.—for all or part of the grains.

Tofu, tempeh, textured vegetable protein, seitan, etc. also make good substitutions for all or part of the grain.

Chopped vegetables such as eggplant, zucchini, broccoli, and asparagus make good additions.

1 tablespoon extra-virgin olive oil
1 to 2 onions, chopped
1 stalk celery, diced
1 carrot, diced
1 bell pepper, diced
3 to 4 cloves garlic, minced
3 cups cooked brown rice
1 cup cooked black or kidney beans
3 tablespoons tahini
2 teaspoons tamari
½ teaspoon basil
½ teaspoon oregano
¼ cup minced fresh cilantro
Salt-free vegetable seasoning, to taste
8 large bell peppers, hollowed out for stuffing

You can change the seasonings to suit your taste. Try paprika, cayenne, thyme, rosemary, cumin, curry, etc. Experiment!

Try peanut butter, almond butter, or cashew butter in place of the tahini.

Skip the tahini and use marinara sauce or chili with the grain or beans.

Mix in or top with dairy or soy cheese, your favorite kind.

Add a few nuts or seeds.

Per serving: Calories 198, Protein 5 g, Fat 5 g, Carbohydrates 33 g

Macaroni and Cheese
Pasta con Queso

Yield: 8 servings

This might be slightly more work than the traditional recipe, but it beats the heck out of any boxed macaroni and cheese you'll ever taste.

1 small red onion, chopped
1 red or green bell pepper, diced
Chiles, roasted, peeled, and minced,
    to taste
1 to 2 cloves garlic, minced
1 tablespoon canola oil or butter
1 pound elbow or other small
    pasta, cooked al dente
½ cup sliced black olives
3 cups grated dairy or soy
    Monterey Jack or cheddar cheese
¼ cup minced fresh cilantro

Preheat the oven to 350°F.

In a large, heavy skillet, sauté the onion, pepper, chiles, and garlic in the oil or butter until tender.

Combine all the ingredients together, and mix well. Place in a casserole or baking dish, and bake uncovered about 25 to 30 minutes, or until the cheese is bubbly and browned on top. Serve hot and enjoy!

Per serving: Calories 260, Protein 14 g, Fat 16 g, Carbohydrates 15 g

Pasta with Lime-Cilantro Sauce and Pine Nuts

Yield: 6 servings

I was first served something very similar to this at a little restaurant, but it was loaded with heavy cream and butter. I liked the idea but went home and played with it until I was satisfied with a lower-fat, nondairy sauce.

In a blender, combine the tofu, scallions, lime juice, garlic, and Parmesan cheese, if using. Blend well. Mix with the cilantro and place in a small saucepan over low heat. Heat gently just for a minute or two, and pour over the hot pasta. Sprinkle with a few pine nuts. Serve and enjoy!

VARIATIONS

Pistachios substitute well for the pine nuts. Crumble a little feta cheese on top.

1 (12.3-ounce) package soft silken tofu
2 scallions, chopped
Juice of 2 limes
2 to 3 cloves garlic, minced
½ cup soy or dairy Parmesan (optional)
⅓ cup minced fresh cilantro
1 pound pasta, cooked al dente
½ cup pine nuts

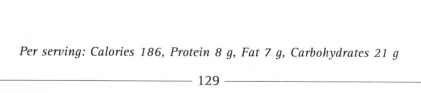

Per serving: Calories 186, Protein 8 g, Fat 7 g, Carbohydrates 21 g

Potato Taco

Yield: 4 servings

This makes a wonderful addition to a combination plate with a Spinach and Walnut Enchiladas, page 125, a Black Bean Burro, page 121, and, of course, Frijoles, page 150, and Spanish rice.

8 taco shells (see below)
2 cups Potatoes, p. 45, or
    Southwest Potato Fritatas, p. 135
2 cups shredded lettuce
1 cup diced tomatoes
1 cup grated soy or dairy cheese
    (optional)
1 cup Guacamole, p. 94 (optional)
1 cup salsa

Preheat the oven to 400°F. If you are using already prepared taco shells, place them on an unoiled baking sheet, and bake for about 5 to 8 minutes just before serving. If you're beginning with soft tortillas, see taco shells below.

Meanwhile, heat the potatoes in a heavy skillet over medium heat. When the potatoes are heated through and the taco shells are warm and crispy, divide the potatoes among the taco shells, and place them in the bottom of each shell. On top of the potatoes, layer the shredded lettuce, tomatoes, cheese, guacamole, and the salsa. Serve two tacos per person with lots of napkins. Enjoy!

TACO SHELLS

There are a number of good commercial taco shells on the market today, some even made with organic corn. However, for something different, you might like to make your own shells. These may be made by either frying or baking the tortillas.

To fry: Heat about a half-inch of canola or olive oil in a large, heavy skillet over medium-high heat. When hot, place a corn or wheat tortilla into the oil. Using a pair of tongs, immediately bend half of the tortilla back over itself in a sort of "U" shape on its side. The bottom half of the "U" should be in the hot oil, and the top half should be held up out of the oil with the tongs. When the half that is in the oil becomes golden brown and crispy, invert the taco, placing the unfried side in the oil. Or, if you prefer, fry the taco flat and layer the ingredients on top of it. A flat taco is generally called a tostada.

To bake: It's a little tricky to bake the shells in an "U" shape in the oven, but with ingenuity it is not impossible. I know one chef who created a little rack out of coat hanger wire to place the shell in while baking. Another idea is to drape the tortilla over the wire grill in the oven so that the sides hang down. The trick then is to bake them so that they can be removed from the rack after becoming crispy. Or, as in the tostada recipe, place the tortilla flat and bake it into a tostada shell. Baked shells, obviously, have less fat than the fried shells.

VARIATIONS

Instead of the potatoes, substitute the Sloppy Joses filling, page 111, Frijoles, page 150, Calabacitas, page 143, or Guacamole, page 94.

For something different, add or substitute grated carrots, jicama or beets, sunflower or alfalfa sprouts, or finely shredded red or green cabbage.

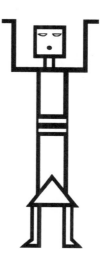

Per serving: Calories 240, Protein 7 g, Fat 2 g, Carbohydrates 48 g

Seitan Fajitas

Yield: 8 fajitas

Hearty and satisfying, serve with rice and beans and shredded greens.

1 large onion, cut into long, thin slices
2 green, yellow, or red bell peppers, cut into thin julienne strips
1 tablespoon olive oil
2 cloves garlic, minced
1 tomato, chopped
1 pound seitan, thinly sliced
1 chile, roasted, peeled, and minced (optional)
1 teaspoon chili powder
1 teaspoon cumin powder
Juice of 2 limes
8 whole wheat tortillas

Sauté the onion and peppers in the olive oil until tender. Add the garlic and tomato, and sauté another 5 minutes. Add the remaining ingredients and cook another 5 to 10 minutes, or until heated through.

Meanwhile, heat the tortillas one at a time in a large, heavy skillet, or wrap a stack of tortillas in a well-dampened but not dripping dish towel, and place in a preheated 350°F oven. Turn off the oven before placing the towel-wrapped tortillas inside, and let the residual heat warm and soften the tortillas.

Wrap the fajita filling in a hot tortilla, and serve. Enjoy!

VARIATIONS

You can also sauté mushrooms, zucchini, corn, eggplant, potatoes, or other vegetables along with the seitan.

Per serving: Calories 206, Protein 22 g, Fat 3 g, Carbohydrates 21 g

Seitan with Ancho Chile Sauce

Yield: 6 servings

Serve with grilled corn on the cob or other grilled veggies—yellow squash, portobello mushrooms, or fresh chiles.

To make the sauce, remove the stems, from the dried chiles. Lightly toast them in a hot, dry skillet, stirring constantly, about 2 to 3 minutes. Place the chiles in a small bowl. Cover with warm water and let soften about 20 minutes. Drain, but save the water.

Combine the softened chiles with the other sauce ingredients in a blender, and blend until very smooth. You want a consistency a little thicker than broth; if too thick, add a little of the reserved soaking water.

To make the marinated seitan, heat the oil and/or wine in a large, heavy skillet over medium-high heat. Lightly sauté the garlic and seitan strips. Add the vegetable stock, vinegar, and tamari, and cook until the liquid has thickened and the seitan is nicely browned.

Lower the heat and add the sauce, stirring together with the seitan to coat. Heat through over low heat until slightly thickened, about 10 to 15 minutes. Serve and enjoy!

VARIATIONS

Grill the seitan strips over mesquite or other grilling wood. Try other chiles.

Add a different flavor by substituting apple, pineapple, or papaya juice for the other sweeteners. Don't let the seitan set too long in the juice, or the enzymes in the pineapple or papaya will break down the protein, and it will fall to pieces.

Ancho Chile Sauce:
4 dried ancho chiles, or 1 tablespoon dried ancho chile powder
⅔ cup vegetable stock
2 to 3 cloves garlic, minced
2 tablespoons tomato paste
1 teaspoon raw honey, granulated sweetener, sorghum, or unsulfured molasses
½ teaspoon dried oregano
2 teaspoons extra-virgin olive oil

Seitan Marinade:
2 tablespoons extra-virgin olive oil and/or ¼ cup red wine (Burgundy works well)
1 clove garlic, finely minced
2 pounds seitan, thinly sliced
1 to 2 tablespoons vegetable stock
½ teaspoon balsamic or red wine vinegar
1 teaspoon tamari (omit if the seitan has already been marinated)

Per serving: Calories 240, Protein 7 g, Fat 2 g, Carbohydrates 48 g

Shiitake and Sun-Dried Tomato Quesadillas

Yield: 4 servings

Sort of a Mexican grilled cheese, quesadillas can be made very plain and simple for a snack or gussied up for a colorful and delicious appetizer or entrée. Here's a very tasty and festive rendition. Be sure to try some of the variations.

4 whole wheat flour tortillas
1 cup grated dairy or soy Monterey
    Jack cheese
Anaheim chiles, roasted, peeled,
    and minced, to taste
¼ cup chopped hydrated sun-dried
    tomatoes
¼ cup minced scallions or shallots
¼ cup minced fresh cilantro

VARIATIONS

Corn or blue corn tortillas substitute well for wheat tortillas and make delicious, smaller quesadillas.

Here are a few suggestions of ingredients you might add—tomato slices; salsa; cooked pinto, black, or kidney beans; sautéed shiitake, oyster, or button mushrooms; Frijoles, page 150; chopped scallions or onions; diced bell peppers; avocado or guacamole (as a raw garnish); diced papaya or mango; crumbled tofu, cooked, shredded tempeh, or seitan.

For vegan quesadillas, use vegan soy cheese or more vegetables and crumbled tofu.

These can be grilled or baked.

To grill, heat a large, heavy skillet or griddle over medium heat. Add ½ teaspoon cold-pressed canola or extra-virgin olive oil. Lay the tortilla in the skillet, and cover one half of the tortilla with about ¼ of the cheese and filling ingredients. Fold the tortilla over. Grill on the first side until the bottom is brown and toasty, then turn and grill on the other side until the bottom is brown and the cheese is melted. Serve hot with shredded lettuce, sprouts, salsa, and/or guacamole. Enjoy!

To bake, preheat the oven to 350°F. Place the tortilla on a baking sheet, cover half with ¼ of the cheese and chiles, and fold the tortilla over. Bake 10 to 15 minutes, or until the cheese is hot and bubbly. Baked quesadillas may not be as brown and crispy as grilled. Serve as above. Enjoy!

Note: For great appetizers, cut the cooked quesadillas into thin wedges, and place on a serving tray with Jicama Fresca, page 50, tomato slices, and a bowl of salsa picante or guacamole.

Per serving: Calories 200, Protein 10 g, Fat 10 g, Carbohydrates 17 g

Southwest Potato Fritatas

Yield: 4 servings

This is sort of a vegan quiche, very flavorful and attractive for brunch or a potluck.

Heat the oil in a large, heavy skillet over medium-high heat. Add the potatoes and green onions, and sauté about 10 minutes, or until the potatoes are fairly browned.

In a bowl, mix the rest of the ingredients together, except the cheese. Pour over the potatoes. Reduce the heat to medium, cover, and cook about 10 minutes. Remove the cover and sprinkle with the grated cheese.

Preheat the oven to broil.

Just before serving, place the entire skillet under the broiler for 3 to 5 minutes, or until the cheese is melted, brown, and bubbly. Serve immediately with warm tortillas. Enjoy!

VARIATIONS

Add other vegetables, beans, or rice to the mixture. Celery, carrots, squash, mushrooms, or peas might be especially tasty.

2 tablespoons olive oil

3 large baked potatoes, cut into ¼-inch slices

1 cup fresh or frozen corn

1 (15-ounce) can ripe olives, drained and sliced

3 green onions, diced

Chiles, peeled, seeded, and minced, to taste

2 tablespoons minced fresh cilantro

½ cup crumbled tofu

Egg replacer equivalent to 3 eggs, p. 24

1 teaspoon chili powder

⅓ cup grated soy or dairy cheddar or Monterey Jack cheese

Per serving: Calories 476, Protein 13 g, Fat 30 g, Carbohydrates 39 g

Stuffed Onions de Sedona

Yield: 4 servings

For best results, look for Vidalia or other seasonal sweet onions. This may also be made to stuff tomatoes, zucchini, eggplant, or winter squash.

4 large sweet onions

½ cup cooked rice
½ cup cooked black or adzuki
  beans
¼ cup chopped hydrated sun-dried
  tomatoes
¼ cup pine nuts
½ teaspoon chili powder
½ teaspoon cumin
Pinch of cayenne (optional)
½ cup whole-grain bread crumbs
¼ cup minced fresh cilantro

½ cup red wine
½ cup vegetable stock

Peel the onions, slice off the tops, and hollow them out, leaving about a ½-inch thick shell.

Steam the shells lightly so they do not lose their shape. Chop the rest of the onions, and set aside for the stuffing.

Preheat the oven to 375°F.

In a bowl, mix together the chopped onions, rice, beans, tomatoes, pine nuts, and seasonings. Spoon into the onion shells, heaping high on top. Sprinkle the tops with the bread crumbs and cilantro. Place in a baking dish, and pour the wine and vegetable stock over the stuffed onions. Bake uncovered 30 to 35 minutes. Serve with a crusty jalapeño bread and a salad. Enjoy!

VARIATIONS

Try a little feta or grated Monterey Jack cheese sprinkled on top before baking.

Sauté some sliced shiitake or button mushrooms, or a couple of cloves of garlic, and mix into the filling.

Scallions or parsley will add a little color and interest as a garnish.

Per serving: Calories 205, Protein 7 g, Fat 5 g, Carbohydrates 32 g

Stuffed Tortilla Pizzas

Yield: 1 serving

This makes a very decadent, but simple, pizza with a Southwestern accent.
Kids especially like this one.

Preheat the oven to 400°F or turn to broil.

Place 1 of the tortillas on an oiled baking sheet. Sprinkle the tortilla evenly with about ⅓ of the grated cheese. Place the other tortilla on top of it. Spread the top tortilla with the salsa and beans.

Top with the remainder of the grated cheese and the vegetarian pepperoni or Canadian bacon, if desired. Garnish the top of the pizza with the minced cilantro. Place the pizza in the oven or under the broiler, and cook until the cheese is melted and browned. (Be especially careful not to burn the pizza if using the broiler.) Serve hot and enjoy!

VARIATIONS

Add fresh chopped vegetables to your pizza—mushrooms, zucchini rounds, onion, bell or jalapeño peppers, even broccoli or asparagus!

Sun-dried tomatoes or artichoke hearts are very tasty additions.

2 whole wheat tortillas

1 cup grated soy or dairy jalapeño, Jack, or cheddar cheese

⅓ cup mild, medium, or hot salsa

⅓ cup cooked pinto, kidney, or black beans

4 to 5 slices vegetarian pepperoni or Canadian bacon, cut into small pieces (optional)

¼ cup finely minced fresh cilantro

Per serving: Calories 516, Protein 37 g, Fat 16 g, Carbohydrates 56 g

Tamale Pie

Yield: 4 servings

This is a delicious casserole, colorful and flavorful. Try some of the variations also.

Crust:

1 cup yellow or blue cornmeal

3 cups water

½ teaspoon chili powder

Filling:

1 red or yellow onion, chopped

2 to 3 cloves garlic, minced

2 cups cooked kidney or pinto beans, cooked

1 cup frozen or fresh corn

½ cup diced green or red bell pepper

½ cup chopped celery

4 mild chiles, roasted, peeled, and diced

½ cup chopped, sliced ripe olives

1 tablespoon extra-virgin olive oil or red wine

2 teaspoons chili powder

½ teaspoon ground cumin

2 tablespoons tomato paste

½ cup grated dairy or soy cheese (optional)

To make the crust, bring 3 cups of water to a boil in a medium saucepan. Slowly add the cornmeal, stirring rapidly with a wire whisk. Cook, continuing to stir often, until the mixture has thickened. Stir in the chili powder.

To make the filling, sauté the onions and garlic in a heavy skillet in the oil or wine until tender. Mix well with the rest of the filling ingredients. Season to taste and set aside.

Preheat the oven to 350°F.

When the cornmeal is thick, spread about half into an oiled 8 x 8-inch baking pan. Spread the filling over that, and top with the remaining cornmeal mixture. Sprinkle with the grated cheese, if desired. Bake for 30 to 40 minutes, or until cooked throughout and the cornmeal/cheese is browned. Serve hot and enjoy!

VARIATIONS

Add other vegetables to the mixture, such as zucchini or yellow squash, eggplant, chopped spinach, sautéed mushrooms, etc.

Substitute anasazi, rattlesnake, tepary, or black turtle beans.

Cooked rice, barley, or posole (hominy) are nice additions.

Sun-dried tomatoes add a rich sweetness.

Use minced fresh cilantro as an ingredient or as a garnish.

Per serving: Calories 376, Protein 12 g, Fat 7 g, Carbohydrates 65 g

Tex-Mex Pasta

Yield: 6 servings

Who says pasta has to be Italian? Here's an interesting and tasty variation with a real "along-the-border tang."

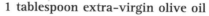

In a large, heavy skillet, heat the oil, and sauté the onions until tender. Add the pepper, chiles, tomatoes, corn, garlic, and chili powder, and sauté another 3 to 5 minutes. Add the beans, cilantro, and lime juice, and cook another 5 minutes. Serve the sauce over pasta garnished, perhaps, with minced cilantro and chopped scallions. Enjoy!

1 tablespoon extra-virgin olive oil
1 red onion, chopped
1 red or green bell pepper, diced
½ cup minced chiles (mild, hot, or a combination of 2 or more varieties)
3 to 4 ripe tomatoes, chopped
⅓ cup fresh or frozen corn kernels (optional)
2 to 3 cloves garlic, minced
1 teaspoon chili powder
1 cup drained, cooked black beans
1 tablespoon minced fresh cilantro
Juice of 1 lime
1 pound semolina or corn pasta, cooked al dente

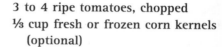

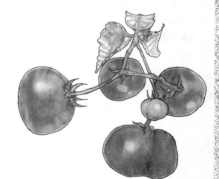

Per serving: Calories 172, Protein 6 g, Fat 3 g, Carbohydrates 30 g

Vegan Mole

Yield: 6 servings

This is a classic mole sauce done vegan and chocolate-free without giving up any of the flavor. Adjust the seasonings to make it as mild or as spicy as you like.

2 cups textured vegetable protein
    chunks
3 cups boiling water
2 tablespoons salsa or barbecue
    sauce (optional)

1 tablespoon extra-virgin olive oil
1 red onion, chopped
2 to 3 cloves garlic, minced
¼ teaspoon cinnamon
Small pinch of cloves
1 to 2 large dried ancho or pasilla
    peppers, crushed in a mortar and
    pestle or blender

4 ripe tomatoes, chopped
¼ cup vegetable broth
1 large flour tortilla, shredded
1 ounce dairy-free carob chips
    (3 tablespoons)
1 teaspoon raw honey or
    granulated sweetener (optional)

In a medium pot, combine the textured vegetable protein, boiling water, and salsa or barbecue sauce, and let set for about 5 minutes. Then simmer over medium-low heat for about 15 to 20 minutes.

Heat a large, heavy skillet over medium-high heat, and add the oil and the onion. Sauté about 5 minutes or until the onion becomes translucent and tender. Add the garlic and sauté another 5 minutes. Add the cinnamon, cloves, and ancho pepper. Stir and add the rest of the ingredients, except the textured vegetable protein. Simmer for 10 to 15 minutes, or until hot throughout and the carob chips are melted.

Purée in small batches until smooth, add the textured vegetable protein mixture, and adjust the seasonings to taste. Serve hot with rice, tortillas, and a light salad. Enjoy!

Per serving: Calories 169, Protein 15 g, Fat 4 g, Carbohydrates 18 g

VEGETABLES AND SIDES

Arugula and Other Greens

Salads and greens make a wonderfully nutritious compliment to hotter dishes, as they tend to cool the palate somewhat.
The spicy leaves of the arugula plant may be broken up into a salad or lightly steamed. They are high in vitamin A and compliment other greens nicely. Try the following recipe as a side dish with black-eyed peas and corn bread.

Steamed Mixed Greens

Yield: 4 servings

6 cups chopped mixed greens—beet greens, arugula, kale, red or green chard, spinach, collards, turnip greens, etc.
1 small onion, sliced
2 tablespoons tamari
½ teaspoon balsamic vinegar

Chop the greens and wash them well in a large colander. While still wet, place them in a large, shallow skillet with the onion. Cover and cook over medium heat, stirring occasionally until soft and tender, about 5 minutes. Toss lightly with the tamari and balsamic vinegar. Serve and enjoy!

VARIATIONS

Diced red bell pepper will add a little color to this dish.

For something different, try a little lime or lemon juice and a couple of cloves of minced garlic.

For something really different, but surprisingly delicious, add 1 very thinly sliced apple and the juice of 1 lemon.

Per serving: Calories 29, Protein 2 g, Fat 0 g, Carbohydrates 5 g

Squash

It's easy to do magic with vegetables. Simply throw a pumpkin into the air and watch it come down squash.

—Zerbo Boillenger

Squash, along with corn and beans, are called the "three sisters" of Southwestern cuisine. This delicious and extremely versatile vegetable is grown and enjoyed world-wide. A common product of home gardens because it grows so well, squash is usually divided into two groups: summer squash and winter squash. Either group can be roasted, baked, steamed, or fried. Here are some specific recipes your family and guests will enjoy.

Calabacitas

People forget the importance of vegetables in Southwestern dining, so here is a delicious reminder. Try calabacitas perhaps wrapped in a wheat or corn tortilla as a burrito or topped with an enchilada sauce and grated soy or dairy cheese.

In a large, heavy skillet, sauté the onions in the oil or braise with the tomatoes until soft and tender. Add the remaining ingredients (except the cheese), cover, and cook about 10 minutes, or until the squash is tender. Top with the cheese, if desired, and serve hot. Enjoy!

VARIATIONS

Sauté some mushrooms (button, shiitake, or portobello) along with the onion. Add about 2 cups of any variety cooked beans to make this a one-pot meal.

½ onion, chopped
1 tablespoon olive oil (optional)
2 tomatoes, chopped
1 cup sliced or chopped zucchini, yellow squash, or other summer squash
½ cup whole kernel corn
1 mild chile, roasted, peeled, and chopped
2 to 3 cloves garlic, minced
¼ cup minced fresh cilantro
1 teaspoon chili powder
Juice of 1 lime
½ cup grated dairy or soy cheese (optional)

Per serving: Calories 128, Protein 4 g, Fat 0 g, Carbohydrates 27 g

Lemon Maple Butternut Squash

Yield: 4 servings

1 medium butternut squash (about 2½ pounds)
3 tablespoons pure maple syrup
2 tablespoons lemon juice
1 teaspoon grated lemon rind

Preheat the oven to 400°F.

Cut the squash in half, and scoop out the seeds and strings from the center. Peel and cut each half into quarters. Steam for 5 minutes.

Place the squash in a lightly oiled casserole dish. Combine the remaining ingredients and pour over the squash. Cover and bake for 25 minutes. Uncover and baste with the juices from the bottom of the dish. Bake, uncovered, another 10 to 15 minutes. Serve hot and enjoy!

Per serving: Calories 154, Protein 2 g, Fat 0 g, Carbohydrates 36 g

Squash and Bell Peppers

Lightly sauté diced summer squash, red onions, garlic, and red and/or green bell peppers in a small amount of olive oil until tender. If desired, add some chopped tomatoes, chopped chiles, diced celery and/or carrots, and a little chopped fresh basil or cilantro. Serve and enjoy!

Stuffed Zucchini Santa Fe

Yield: 4 servings

These are quite simple and elegant, perfect for a special dinner. Serve with a salad, black beans, and corn bread.

Preheat the oven to 350°F.

In a small skillet, toast the pumpkin seeds over low heat until they brown and pop. Remove from the skillet and set aside. Add a little stock or oil to the hot skillet, and sauté the chopped zucchini until tender. Mix into the rice.

Spoon about ⅓ cup of the rice/zucchini mixture into each hollowed out zucchini "boat," and place on an oiled baking pan. Bake, uncovered, for about 30 minutes. Sprinkle with the cheese and pumpkin seeds, and bake another 10 minutes. Serve hot and enjoy!

VARIATIONS

Substitute yellow squash or eggplant for the zucchini.

Add beans, mushrooms, sun-dried tomatoes, artichoke hearts, etc. to the stuffing mixture. Be creative!

Substitute barley, corn, bulgur wheat, or other grain for the rice.

¼ cup raw pumpkin seeds (pepitos)

1 tablespoon olive oil or stock for sautéing

4 medium zucchini, cut in half lengthwise and hollowed out (Save what you scoop out for the stuffing.)

3 cups Spanish Rice, p. 152

1 cup grated soy or dairy cheese (Monterey Jack, cheddar, or jalapeño)

Per serving: Calories 359, Protein 14 g, Fat 12 g, Carbohydrates 46 g

Sweet Squash with Pine Nuts

Yield: 4 servings

2 acorn, delacourt, or butternut
   squashes, halved and seeded
½ cup pine nuts
1 small apple, chopped
¼ cup raisins
Juice and grated peel of 1 small
   orange
1½ tablespoons raw honey or
   brown rice syrup
1 tablespoon canola oil (optional)

Preheat the oven to 375°F.

Place the squash in an oiled casserole dish. Mix the remaining ingredients together, and place in the hollow cavity of the squash halves. Cover and bake until very tender, about 35 to 45 minutes. Serve hot and enjoy!

Per serving: Calories 272, Protein 6 g, Fat 9 g, Carbohydrates 42 g

Zucchini Mexicali

Yield: 4 servings

This is a quick and simple side dish. You can also add beans and serve with corn bread for a simple meal.

4 medium zucchini
2 tablespoons olive oil
½ cup grated Monterey Jack cheese
   or soy Jack cheese
1 to 2 cloves garlic, minced
¼ cup finely minced cilantro

Preheat the oven to 375°F.

Slice the zucchini lengthwise, place in an oiled baking dish, and sprinkle lightly with the olive oil and the dairy or soy cheese, garlic, and cilantro. Bake about 25 to 30 minutes, or until nicely tender. Serve and enjoy!

VARIATION

Use a combination of zucchini and yellow crookneck squash. Add a little finely diced red onion and some red and green sweet bell peppers. Add the olive oil and, if desired, Parmesan cheese instead of the Jack cheese. Bake as above. Serve and enjoy!

Per serving: Calories 138, Protein 5 g, Fat 11 g, Carbohydrates 5 g

Broiled Tex-Mex Tomatoes

Yield: 4 servings

These are quick and simple, and make a nice accompaniment to grilled tofu or seitan. In fact, these can be done on the grill as well as under the broiler.

4 large, ripe tomatoes
1 cup grated Monterey Jack or soy Jack cheese
½ cup minced fresh cilantro
Dash of hot sauce (optional)

Core the tomatoes, cut in half, and place the halves on an oiled baking sheet. Top each with the grated cheese, minced cilantro, and a dash of hot sauce, if desired. Place under a broiler and broil for 5 to 7 minutes, or until the cheese is melted, brown, and bubbly. Serve and enjoy!

Per serving: Calories 132, Protein 8 g, Fat 7 g, Carbohydrates 5 g

Santa Fe Steamed Kale

Yield: 6 servings

This makes a great side dish with beans or spicy stews.

Wash the kale very well, leave wet, and place in a large, heavy skillet. Add the garlic and tamari, cover, and cook over medium heat for about 10 minutes, stirring once. (The kale will steam in the water left on the leaves.) Add black pepper and hot sauce to taste. Serve hot and enjoy!

1 pound kale, washed and finely shredded (about 12 cups)
1 to 2 cloves garlic, minced
1 tablespoon tamari
Black pepper, to taste (optional)
Dash of hot sauce or pinch of cayenne (optional)

VARIATIONS

A slice of red onion on top is very nice.

For a different flavor, add other chopped greens—chard, spinach, collards, mustard, beet greens, or turnip greens.

Per serving: Calories 37, Protein 2 g, Fat 0 g, Carbohydrates 6 g

Steamed Chard with Pine Nuts

Yield: 4 servings

Pine nuts add a nice touch to the steamed greens.

1 pound chard (about 12 cups
    chopped)
2 tablespoons tamari
⅓ cup pine nuts
Dash of hot sauce (optional)

Wash the chard well and chop slightly, removing any large, thick pieces of stem. Place in a large skillet with a tight fitting lid. Splash with the tamari and sprinkle with the pine nuts. Cover and cook slowly over medium heat, stirring 2 to 3 times, for about 10 minutes, or until the chard is limp and cooked throughout. Serve hot and enjoy, with a dash of hot sauce, if desired.

Per serving: Calories 78, Protein 4 g, Fat 5 g, Carbohydrates 4 g

Steamed Sweet Potatoes and Oranges

Yield: 4 servings

Oranges grow well throughout the Southwest and add a delightful flavor to many dishes. This unusual combination is a little different, perhaps, but it will soon win you over.

2 large sweet potatoes, peeled and
    chopped coarsely
2 oranges, peeled, seeded, and
    chopped
Pinch of ground cardamom
⅓ cup raisins or currants
¼ cup orange juice
1 teaspoon sorghum, unsulfured
    molasses, or maple syrup
    (optional)
½ cup pecan halves

Steam the sweet potatoes until almost cooked through. Combine with the remaining ingredients (except the pecans) in a heavy skillet, cover, and cook over medium heat until thick and the sweet potatoes are thoroughly cooked. Serve hot sprinkled with pecans. Enjoy!

VARIATIONS

Substitute apples or pears for the oranges, apple juice for the orange juice, cinnamon for the cardamom, and walnuts for the pecans.

Per serving: Calories 326, Protein 3 g, Fat 8 g, Carbohydrates 59 g

Sunshine Dilled Carrots

Yield: 4 servings

Whether you like carrots or not, you'll love carrots prepared like this! Lightly sweetened with the sunshine of Southwestern oranges, a hint of dill, and garlic, this is also very simple to prepare.

Steam the carrots for a few minutes, but leave them slightly crunchy. In a large, heavy skillet, sauté the onion and garlic in the oil about 5 minutes or until tender. Add the carrots and the rest of the ingredients, and cook another 5 to 7 minutes, or until well heated throughout. Garnish with a little minced parsley or toasted sesame seeds, and serve hot. Enjoy!

VARIATIONS

You may always add other vegetables or substitute for the carrots.

Try green beans, broccoli, cauliflower, snow peas, or whatever sounds tasty to you.

For an interesting flavor, add 1 teaspoon pure maple syrup, ½ teaspoon balsamic vinegar, some minced mint leaves, a finely chopped orange, or some fresh pineapple.

6 to 8 large carrots, sliced
    diagonally
½ onion, chopped
2 cloves garlic, minced
1 teaspoon toasted sesame oil
½ cup orange juice concentrate
1 teaspoon fresh dill
Dash of tamari
Minced fresh parsley or toasted
    sesame seeds, for garnish

Per serving: Calories 130, Protein 2 g, Fat 1 g, Carbohydrates 27 g

Frijoles
Refried Beans

Yield: 4 servings

Double or triple this recipe, and keep some extra frijoles on hand in the freezer. These also make a great bean dip.

1 cup dry beans (pinto, kidney, black, or anasazi)
1 tomato, chopped
1 onion, chopped
2 to 3 cloves garlic, minced
1 tablespoon chili powder
1 tablespoon cumin powder
Mild or hot chiles, to taste
2 tablespoons finely minced fresh cilantro
Salt-free vegetable seasoning, to taste
¼ cup finely chopped fresh epazote (optional)

Sort through the beans, picking out rocks, etc. Soak the beans in enough water to cover well for at least 8 hours or overnight. (A crock-pot or slow-cooker is a real time-saver when cooking beans, and it's convenient to use for soaking as well.) Discard the soaking water and cover with fresh, cold water. Bring to a boil, then reduce the heat to medium. Cover and cook for at least 1 hour. The beans should be very soft and tender. If they are mealy or crunchy, continue cooking, adding more water if needed. (Caution: Never add salt or anything containing salt to beans until they are completely cooked. Salted beans may not cook all the way through.)

When the beans are done, add the remaining ingredients and cook, uncovered, until the vegetables are tender and the beans start to thicken a little. Add the epazote, if desired. Mash well with a potato masher or in a food processor. Adjust the seasonings to taste. Serve topped with grated cheddar, Monterey Jack, soy jalapeño, soy mozzarella, crumbled tofu, shredded lettuce, guacamole, salsa, chopped onions, etc., with a stack of hot whole wheat or corn tortillas on the side. Or use for burritos, huevos rancheros, quesadillas, etc. Enjoy!

Per serving: Calories 168, Protein 8 g, Fat 0 g, Carbohydrates 32 g

Ranch Fries

Yield: 6 servings

These delicious, crispy potatoes are actually not "fried" at all, they're baked. Great for kids of all ages. Try them with Spicy Tomato Catch-Up, page 95.

Preheat the oven to 350°F. Cut the potatoes into your favorite "French fry" shapes—cottage fries, shoestring, crinkle-cut, chips, etc.

Lightly oil a baking sheet with cold-pressed canola oil. Spread the cut potatoes on the baking sheet. Sprinkle with your favorite vegetable seasoning—herbs, garlic or onion powder, chili powder, etc.—to taste.

Bake until the potatoes start to become golden brown. Raise the oven temperature to 400°F, and continue baking until the "fries" are as crunchy as you like. Some people like them barely done, and others like them very dark and crispy. Serve hot and enjoy!

Note: The length of time for cooking will vary according to the size and shape you've cut the potatoes into. Remember that shoestrings will cook faster and be crispier than cottage fries. To keep the potatoes from becoming too dry, place a pan of water in the oven.

VARIATION

Try sweet potato "fries."

4 to 5 baking potatoes, scrubbed
  but not peeled
Cold-pressed canola oil
Your favorite vegetable seasonings,
  to taste

Per serving: Calories 197, Protein 3 g, Fat 2 g, Carbohydrates 43 g

Spanish Rice Casserole

Yield: 4 servings

Serve this as a tasty side dish for a Mexican fiesta, or add a few more vegetables and a little extra cheese and make it the main course.

2 cups long-grain brown rice
4 cups vegetable stock or water
1 onion, chopped
1 sweet bell pepper, diced
3 to 4 tomatoes, chopped
Mild or hot chiles, to taste
2 to 3 cloves garlic, minced
1 tablespoon chili powder
1 teaspoon cumin powder
2 tablespoons cilantro

½ cup grated Monterey Jack or soy
   jalapeño cheese

Preheat the oven to 350°F.

In a large bowl, mix everything except the cheese. Pour into a large casserole dish, cover, and bake for 45 to 50 minutes. Remove the lid and sprinkle the top with the cheese. Bake another 5 to 10 minutes, or until the cheese is hot and bubbly. Serve with hot tortillas and frijoles. Enjoy!

VARIATIONS

Chopped, rehydrated sun-dried tomatoes add a nice flavor.

Substitute ½ cup tomato sauce for ½ cup of stock.

Per serving: Calories 330, Protein 10 g, Fat 6 g, Carbohydrates 59 g

GRILLING AND COOKOUTS

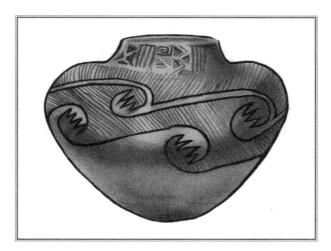

A Vegetarian Cookout!

Who says vegetarians can't enjoy barbecue? Ever since Cro-Magnon man first cooked his root vegetables over an outdoor fire, there has been such a variety of grillable vegetarian fare that it's difficult to understand how barbecue became so synonymous with animal flesh. Besides the veggie burgers and tofu wieners, many new cookbooks, vegetarian and otherwise, have recently been shouting the praises of grilled fresh vegetables and even fruits. (Try grilling fresh pineapple rings—yum!) Here, then, are a variety of meatless ways you and your family can celebrate the joys of outdoor grilling and dining.

Meatless Meats

For those to whom barbecue simply means "meat" and nothing but, there are now a number of very tasty (and much more nutritious) meat substitutes. Vegetarian burgers, cutlets, tofu wieners, tempeh bacon, veggie sausage links, and patties are all designed to give you that familiar taste and texture without the cholesterol, fat, or cruelty associated with their meat counterparts. Experiment with different products until you find ones you enjoy.

Barbecued Tempeh or Seitan

Yield: 4 servings

Light the grill and don your funniest barbecue apron, gather the family in the backyard, and enjoy some finger-lickin' good barbecue without animal products!

Marinade:
1 cup vegetable stock or juice
1 tablespoon tamari
2 to 3 cloves garlic, minced
Pinch of freshly ground black
    pepper (optional)
Dash of Tabasco (optional)

2 pounds tempeh, sliced ½ inch
    thick
 or
4 tempeh burgers
 or
2 pounds seitan, sliced or whole

1 cup Salsa de Barbacoa, p. 90, or
    your favorite barbecue sauce

Mix all the marinade ingredients together, and pour over the tempeh or seitan. Let marinate several hours or overnight.

Light the barbecue grill and let it burn until the coals are white-grey all over. Place the tempeh or seitan on the grill, and cook about 5 to 10 minutes on each side, or until hot, browned, and grilled.

Brush with barbecue sauce and cook another 5 minutes on each side, brushing with more sauce as needed. Serve hot and enjoy!

Per serving: Calories 534, Protein 38 g, Fat 15 g, Carbohydrates 60 g

Grilled Mushrooms

Yield: 4 servings

Grilling somehow mellows the sharp herbs in this marinade. Try this also with other vegetables. Serve over toast, rice, or baked potatoes.

In a large bowl, combine the oil, vinegar, garlic, shallot, chives, and parsley, and stir well. Add the mushrooms and toss lightly to coat. Marinate the mushrooms in the refrigerator for at least 3 hours.

Meanwhile, soak wooden skewers in water for about 30 minutes. This will keep them from burning over the hot fire. Prepare your grill and get the coals hot.

Skewer the mushrooms and grill, turning often, until the mushrooms are cooked through, about 8 to 10 minutes, depending on the mushrooms and size. Serve hot and enjoy!

VARIATIONS

Add other vegetables to the skewers, sliced zucchini, cherry tomatoes, pearl onions, pieces of red or green bell pepper, or cloves of elephant garlic.

Cubed tofu or seitan may be quite tasty.

For something very different, add pieces of pear, apple, orange, pineapple, etc., to the skewer. Cut the fruit in pieces large enough that they won't break and fall off the skewer.

Try other marinades or alter some of the ingredients in this one. For example, try another flavor of vinegar, another type of oil, or other herbs. Try the following combination, especially for a tropical flavor: ½ cup fruit-sweetened jam, 1 teaspoon umeboshi plum paste, and 1 teaspoon tamari.

Marinade:

½ cup extra-virgin olive oil

2 tablespoons balsamic vinegar

2 cloves garlic, minced

1 small shallot, minced

2 tablespoons minced fresh chives

2 tablespoons minced fresh parsley or cilantro

2 pounds total of at least 3 varieties of fresh mushrooms—button, shiitake, portobello, porcini, oyster, etc.—cleaned and trimmed

Per serving: Calories 183, Protein 3 g, Fat 13 g, Carbohydrates 10 g

Grilled Tofu

Yield: 4 servings

A delicious and beautiful dish to serve company, with or without barbecue sauce.

2 pounds firm tofu

Marinade:
¼ cup tamari
2 to 4 cloves garlic, minced
½ cup vegetable stock
½ teaspoon ginger juice, p. 41
1 teaspoon extra-virgin olive oil
   (optional)
Dash of Tabasco (optional)
Dash of liquid smoke (optional)
Pinch of freshly ground black
   pepper
Salt-free vegetable seasoning, to
   taste

In a large steamer basket, steam the tofu for 20 to 30 minutes. This will make the tofu firmer and give it a nice texture for grilling.

Place the steamed tofu in a shallow pan, and pour the marinade over it. Let it marinate several hours or overnight.

Grill over hot coals about 5 to 10 minutes on a side, basting either with the marinade or your favorite barbecue sauce. Serve hot and enjoy!

VARIATIONS

Add a little wine or beer to the marinade.

Try a little balsamic vinegar or lemon juice in the marinade.

Serve smothered in sautéed mushrooms and/or onions.

Season with minced fresh parsley or cilantro.

Per serving: Calories 183, Protein 18 g, Fat 9 g, Carbohydrates 5 g

Mt. Lemmon Camper's Stew

Yield: 6 servings

This will easily satisfy the hungriest camper. Make a big Dutch oven full of this stew at your next camp-out, and watch it disappear.

Combine all the ingredients, except the cornstarch and cilantro, in a Dutch oven or large, heavy pot with a cover. Add enough water or vegetable stock to cover. Cook over the campfire, stirring often, until all the vegetables are tender and cooked throughout. In a cup or bowl, stir the cornstarch or arrowroot into 1 cup vegetable stock or water. To this mixture, add about ½ cup of hot broth from the stew, and mix well. Stir this mixture into the cooking stew, and continue cooking and stirring until thick and hot. Adjust the seasonings to taste, and add the cilantro or parsley for garnish. Serve with thick slices of bread or sourdough biscuits, and enjoy!

VARIATIONS

Add any other vegetables you have handy—zucchini, mushrooms, chard, parsnips, bell peppers, chiles, corn, peas, etc.

Other herbs and seasonings will add flavor; try fresh basil, sage, rosemary, etc. Chili powder or hot chiles will add a little zip!

For something deliciously different, add sun-dried tomatoes, artichoke hearts, or a dash of balsamic vinegar.

2 cups textured vegetable protein chunks
1 onion, chopped
2 stalks celery, chopped
2 carrots, chopped
4 to 5 tomatoes, chopped
2 potatoes, chopped
2 turnips, chopped
2 to 3 cloves garlic, minced
⅓ cup tamari
1 bottle ale, stout, or beer, preferably dark and strongly flavored (optional)
Salt and black pepper, to taste
1 tablespoon oregano or thyme

½ cup cornstarch or arrowroot
Chopped cilantro or parsley, for garnish

Per serving: Calories 223, Protein 16 g, Fat 0 g, Carbohydrates 37 g

Roasted Potatoes and Corn

Yield: 4 servings

While the coals are nice and hot, put them to double service. Not only can they grill the food on top of the grill, they can cook potatoes and corn that have been wrapped in foil and nestled among the hot coals.

4 large baking potatoes
4 ears fresh corn on the cob

Wrap the potatoes and corn in aluminum foil, and place down in the hot coals. Turn every 4 to 5 minutes, and cook the potatoes until they give slightly when squeezed in the center. (Use oven mitts so you don't burn your hand.) Cook the corn about 10 to 15 minutes. Try serving the corn lightly spread with umeboshi plum paste instead of butter and salt for a delightfully different taste. Enjoy!

Per serving: Calories 204, Protein 3 g, Fat 0 g, Carbohydrates 47 g

Skillet Bread

Yield: 1 loaf (6 servings)

This simple, versatile bread does not require an oven. It can be made on your stove-top or, better yet, over an open campfire.

In a large bowl, mix together the flour and baking powder. Add the milk and stir with a wooden spoon until the mixture is spongy. Heat one tablespoon of the oil in a 10-inch skillet. (Cast-iron works very well.) Keep the heat low and do not burn.

Add the batter to the skillet, and cook about 15 minutes, or until the bottom is golden brown. Use a large spatula to lift and turn the bread very carefully. I've developed a technique using two large plates. Place 1 plate top down on top of the bread. Invert the skillet and plate so the plate is now on the bottom and skillet is on top. Lift the skillet off and add the remaining tablespoon of oil to it. Place another plate on what is now the top of the bread so that it's sandwiched between two plates. Invert again. Remove the top plate. Now place the skillet back on top, and invert one last time. The bread should now be turned over in the skillet without falling apart. This takes a little practice, but, believe me, it can be done by one person. Cook another 15 minutes. This bread works best if the dough is a little stiff and thick. It's sort of like a giant pancake. Serve with stew or beans, and enjoy!

2 cups whole wheat flour
4 teaspoons non-aluminum baking powder
1¼ cups skim milk or soymilk
2 tablespoons cold-pressed canola oil

VARIATIONS

The addition of 1 egg will help it hold together a little better, or see page 24 about using egg replacers.

You may also substitute buttermilk or soured skim milk or soymilk. Decrease the baking powder to 1 teaspoon and add 1 teaspoon baking soda.

Per serving: Calories 195, Protein 7 g, Fat 6 g, Carbohydrates 29 g

Sonoran Tofu Jerky

Yield: 6 servings

This works better in a food dehydrator, but an oven will work in a pinch. This is a great hiking or backpacking treat. Try some of the variations.

3 pounds firm tofu
3 cups tamari
1 teaspoon liquid smoke
2 tablespoons sorghum or
    unsulfured molasses

Cut the tofu into ¼-inch thick strips, and place in a shallow baking pan.

In another bowl, mix together the tamari, liquid smoke, and molasses. Pour over the tofu and let marinate several hours or overnight.

Preheat the oven to 300°F. Place the pan containing the marinated tofu on the center rack of the oven. After ½ hour, reduce the oven temperature to 250°F, and let dry for 8 hours, or until everything is chewy and very dark brown. Enjoy!

VARIATIONS

For a spicier jerky, add cayenne, Tabasco, or other hot seasoning to the marinade. Try using the juice from a jar or can of jalapeños.

Onion, garlic, mustard, or other flavors and seasonings might add some interest.

Add ¼ cup tomato paste to the marinade.

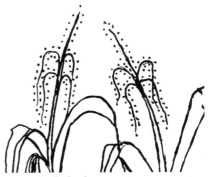

Per serving: Calories 284, Protein 29 g, Fat 9 g, Carbohydrates 18 g

Southwest Grilled Veggies

Yield: 4 servings

Your barbecue grill certainly is not just for meats, and don't limit yourself only to tofu hot dogs and tempeh burgers either. Bell peppers, fresh chiles, corn on the cob, tomatoes, eggplant slices, large onion slices or quarters, and large slices of squash (summer or winter varieties), are all wonderful when grilled. Marinate the vegetables with this tasty sauce for a couple of hours before grilling.

Place all of the vegetables in a shallow pan, and pour the marinade over them. Let set for an hour, or refrigerate and marinate longer (up to 12 hours). Grill the vegetables until tender, basting often. You will need to peel the chiles after grilling, as the peels are not very digestible. Enjoy!

4 cups mixed vegetables in large pieces—peppers cut into quarters and seeded, tomatoes halved, corn on the cob cut into 1-inch rounds, onions quartered, etc. (Include several fresh chiles, to taste.)

Marinade:
½ cup water
1 teaspoon tamari (optional)
1 tablespoon tomato paste
½ teaspoon balsamic vinegar
2 cloves garlic, minced
½ teaspoon chili powder
Pinch of cumin
½ teaspoon lime juice
1 tablespoon finely minced fresh cilantro
Dash of liquid smoke (optional)

Per serving: Calories 63, Protein 2 g, Fat 0 g, Carbohydrates 13 g

Veggie Kabobs

Yield: 4 servings

Simple and elegant, this is a beautiful dish for guests. Use the marinade recipe included here, the Salsa de Barbacoa, page 90, or any one of your favorite marinades.

4 cups mixed vegetables, cut into pieces large enough to fit on a skewer, such as:
Whole button mushrooms
Whole small shiitakes or large mushrooms, cut in half
2-inch pieces of red or green bell pepper
Whole pearl onions or red onions, cut into quarters
Zucchini or yellow squash rounds
Cherry tomatoes or tomato quarters
Corn on the cob, cut into 1-inch rounds
1-inch carrot rounds
Small whole potatoes, cooked until almost done
Brussels sprouts
Artichoke hearts

2 cups of any of the following:
Firm tofu, cut into large cubes
Chunks of seitan
Tofu hot dogs, cut into 2-inch pieces
2-inch cubes of tempeh

2 cups fruit (optional)
2-inch fresh pineapple chunks
Peach or apricot halves

Soak about 12 wooden skewers in water for ½ hour or longer, so they won't burn over the hot coals. Place all the ingredients on the skewers, alternating varieties and colors. Baste with marinade and refrigerate 1 hour or longer.

Light the grill and let the coals burn until completely white all around. Place the kabobs on the grill, and cook, turning very carefully every 5 minutes or so. Baste often with the marinade. Grill until the vegetables are crunchy-tender and heated well throughout. Serve over rice or with baked potatoes. Enjoy!

VARIATIONS

Instead of threading on skewers, cut the vegetables into larger, pieces such as half tomatoes or zucchini quartered lengthwise, marinate, and grill.

Substitute other marinades—barbecue sauce, Italian dressing, etc.

Add a dash of Tabasco or hot sauce.

Marinade:
1 cup fruit-sweetened mango, apricot, or pineapple jam
½ cup frozen apple or pineapple juice concentrate
¼ cup water
1 tablespoon tamari
1 tablespoon umeboshi plum paste

Per serving: Calories 425, Protein 11 g, Fat 5 g, Carbohydrates 82 g

DESSERTS

Basic Whole Wheat Pie Crust

Yield: one 9-inch crust (8 servings)

This is another case where I've often been told that it's "simply not possible to make a good flaky pie crust without shortening or lard, without salt, and using whole wheat flour instead of white." Here's your chance to do the impossible! The following tips make it easier, but experiment, try it a few times, substitute other flours (oat flour, spelt flour, etc.), and find out what works best for you.

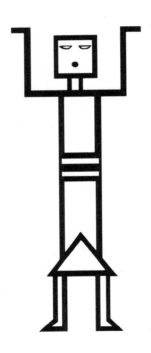

1½ cups whole wheat pastry flour
⅓ cup cold-pressed canola oil
3 to 4 tablespoons ice water

Preheat the oven to 375°F.

Measure the flour into a medium-size mixing bowl. Drizzle the oil into the flour a little at a time, and mix well with a fork after each addition. You will know when you have enough oil when the mixture resembles a bowlful of large crumbs.

Add ice water, 1 tablespoon at a time, mixing very well between each addition. When the dough forms easily into a cohesive and firm ball, you've added enough water.

On a well-floured surface, roll the dough out into a round shape about ¼-inch thick. If the crust does not hold together well, gather it up, return it to the bowl, and add another tablespoon of ice water. Roll it out again. Do not push down too much with the rolling pin. Just let the weight of the rolling pin determine the pressure. After each couple of rolls, lightly pat the surface with a dusting of flour, and turn the crust over, dusting that side also very lightly. This prevents the dough from sticking to the table or the rolling pin.

Another method you might find easier is to roll the dough between two sheets of wax paper. This also makes it simpler to transfer it to the pie pan.

After the dough is rolled, gently transfer it to an oiled pie pan. With your hands, shape it to the contours of the pan. If it tears, just repair it by pushing the dough toward the tear. Cut off the excess dough from the outside of the pan, or, if preferred, just crimp or push the dough up to form a small ridge around the edge of the pie pan. A pretty touch is to take a fork, dip it into water to prevent sticking, and press it diagonally all around the outside edge of the crust.

Remember, if you're not satisfied with the way the crust is turning out on the first try, simply reshape it into a ball, and roll it out again until you are happy with the results. Practice—it will become easier!

If baking the shell with the pie filling (as in pumpkin or apple pie, for instance), just fill and bake according to the recipe. If using with a non-bake recipe, prebake the shell for 10 to 15 minutes, or until brown and firm. Fill according to the recipe you are using. Enjoy!

VARIATIONS

Try this with other flours, finely ground nuts, or a combination of the two. Keep in mind that nuts will most likely not hold together as well as flour. (As a matter of fact, some flours will also tend to be a bit crumbly.) You may need to combine the nuts with a little whole wheat pastry flour or other sticky flour. Also, adjust the oil and water as described in the tips.

Other variations include substituting wheat germ, sesame seeds, or ground sunflower seeds.

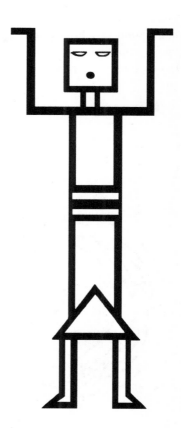

Per serving: Calories 150, Protein 3 g, Fat 9 g, Carbohydrates 15 g

Graham Cracker or Crumb Crust

Yield: one 9-inch crust (8 servings)

Whole-grain cookie crumbs, graham cracker crumbs, etc., all work well in this recipe. It does not require rolling and is a good recipe for beginners who want a successful crust on their first attempt.

2 cups fine graham cracker or cookie crumbs

1 tablespoon raw honey or brown rice syrup

5 tablespoons cold-pressed canola oil

If the crust needs to be prebaked, preheat the oven to 325°F.

In a medium mixing bowl, combine all the ingredients together, and mix thoroughly. If desired, reserve ½ cup of the crumbs for a topping. Press the remaining mixture evenly into the bottom and sides of an oiled 9-inch pie pan. Prebake or bake along with the filling as needed for the recipe you are using. Enjoy!

VARIATION

Grape Nuts cereal, chopped nuts, date sugar, etc., all make tasty additions to the crust. Adjust the sweetness and consistency to suit your taste.

Per serving: Calories 203, Protein 2 g, Fat 10 g, Carbohydrates 24 g

Banana Cream Pie

Yield: one 9-inch pie (8 servings)

Very simple! No baking, except for the crust! There are many variations to this one; try them all.

In a blender, mix the tofu, bananas, sweetener, and vanilla. Pour into the pre-baked pie shell, and refrigerate. Serve chilled and enjoy!

2 cups crumbled firm silken tofu
4 ripe bananas
1 cup raw honey or 1¼ cups granulated sweetener
Dash of pure vanilla
1 (9-inch) pre-baked Whole Wheat Crust, pp. 164-65, or Graham Cracker Crust, p. 166

CAROB CREAM PIE

In a double boiler, melt 1 cup carob chips, and blend with the tofu, sweetener, and vanilla. Eliminate the bananas, or serve as carob-banana cream pie.

COCONUT CREAM PIE

Omit the bananas and add 2 cups unsweetened coconut to the mixture. (Note: You may lightly toast the coconut in a large, heavy, dry skillet if desired.)

Strawberry Cream Pie (or other fruit pie): Substitute strawberries or other fruit for the bananas. Cook 1 tablespoon agar flakes (vegetarian gelatin) in ¼ cup water for five minutes, then add immediately to the tofu mixture, and blend. Increase the sweetener by ¼ cup.

VANILLA CREAM PIE

Omit the bananas and increase the vanilla to 1½ tablespoons.

NUT BUTTER CREAM PIE

Substitute 1 cup peanut, almond, or cashew butter for the bananas.

MANGO CREAM PIE

Alright, here's a real Southwestern version of this simple pie. Simply substitute 3 cups ripe, peeled mangoes for the bananas, and add just a pinch of cinnamon.

LEMON OR LIME PIE

Omit the bananas, increase the sweetener by ¼ cup, and add ⅓ cup of fresh lemon or lime juice.

For a different flavor, try different sweeteners—Sucanat, date sugar, or a combination of 2 or 3 different types of sweeteners.

Per serving: Calories 380, Protein 8 g, Fat 11 g, Carbohydrates 61 g

Pecan Pie

Yield: one 9-inch pie (8 servings)

Pecans grow well in many parts of the Southwest and are plentiful right after harvest.

¼ cup cold-pressed canola oil
½ cup crumbled firm tofu
¼ cup warmed raw honey or
   brown rice syrup
½ cup pure maple syrup
1 teaspoon pure vanilla
1 tablespoon whole wheat flour
2 cups pecan halves
1 (9-inch) Whole Wheat Pie Crust,
   pp. 164–65

Preheat the oven to 350°F.

In a large mixing bowl or blender, combine the oil, tofu, honey, and maple syrup. Mix well. Add the vanilla and flour, and mix again.

Put the pecans into the pie shell, pour the tofu mixture over them, and bake for 30 to 40 minutes, or until a knife inserted in the center comes out clean. Serve warm or cold. Enjoy!

Per serving: Calories 483, Protein 5 g, Fat 32 g, Carbohydrates 42 g

Sweet Potato Pie

Yield: two 9-inch pies (8 servings)

3½ cups steamed, peeled sweet
   potatoes
4 (12.3-ounce) packages extra-firm
   silken tofu
1½ cups raw honey, or 1¾ cups
   granulated sweetener
½ cup sorghum or unsulfured
   molasses
1 tablespoon cinnamon
1 teaspoon allspice
½ teaspoon nutmeg
Pinch of cloves
2 (9-inch) Whole Wheat Pie Crusts,
   pp. 164–65
Pecan halves, for garnish (optional)

Preheat the oven to 350°F.

Combine all the ingredients, except for the crusts and pecans, together in a food processor, in several batches in a blender, or by hand using a large whisk. Pour into the pie shells, and bake for 45 to 50 minutes. Garnish, if desired, with pecan halves. Serve hot and enjoy!

VARIATIONS

Substitute fresh or canned pumpkin or butternut squash.

Per serving: Calories 369, Protein 9 g, Fat 11 g, Carbohydrates 59 g

Tofu Cheesecake

Yield: 6 servings

Here's a delicious cheesecake recipe without the cheese! Don't tell and no one will know, it tastes that rich and creamy.

Preheat the oven to 350°F.

Combine everything, except the crust, in a blender until smooth and creamy. Pour into the prepared crust, and bake for 1 hour. Top, if desired, with fresh strawberries, blueberries, kiwi slices, pineapple, etc. Use several fruits and make into a nice pattern. Garnish with fresh mint leaves. Serve and enjoy!

Variations:

Chopped walnuts or sliced almonds make a nice addition to the top of the cheesecake.

Add some chopped fruit to the filling before baking.

Add 1 cup or more melted carob chips for a carob cheesecake.

2 (12.3-ounce) packages extra-firm tofu
1 (8-ounce) package soy cream cheese
⅓ cup cold-pressed canola oil
1 cup granulated sweetener or ⅞ cup raw honey
3½ tablespoons lemon juice
1 tablespoon pure vanilla

1 (9-inch) Graham Cracker Crust, p. 166, or use your favorite

Per serving: Calories 618, Protein 12 g, Fat 33 g, Carbohydrates 70 g

Tofu Whipped Cream

Yield: about 1 cup

Although I haven't been able to make it form peaks and stand firm like dairy whipped cream, the flavor is excellent and it makes a plain dessert pretty decadent!

2 (12.3-ounce) packages extra-firm silken tofu
⅓ cup raw honey, maple syrup, or brown rice syrup
1 teaspoon pure vanilla

Using an electric mixer and a chilled glass or ceramic bowl, gently blend all the ingredients together, then whip on high speed until aerated and somewhat stiff. Enjoy!

Note: For a little more stiffness, whip in a teaspoon of margarine or butter, and refrigerate before serving.

LEMON WHIP

Add the juice of 1 lemon and 1 teaspoon agar (a vegetarian jelling agent) to the above recipe. Refrigerate before serving.

Instead of lemon juice, substitute lime or orange juice, fresh strawberries, blueberries, or a ripe banana.

BUTTERSCOTCH WHIP

Add 2 tablespoons melted butter or margarine and 1 tablespoon sorghum or unsulfured molasses.

Per 2 tablespoons: Calories 94, Protein 6 g, Fat 2 g, Carbohydrates 12 g

Date-Pecan Pudding

Yield: 6 servings

This dessert may be sweet and taste sinful, but it's jam-packed with nutrients. No need to feel guilty, just enjoy!

In a medium saucepan, stir the water into the flour, whisking well. Cook over medium-low heat, and simmer for 30 minutes, stirring often.

Pour ½ of the mixture into a blender with the dates, and blend until creamy. Remove to a bowl. Pour the remainder of the mixture into the blender with the pecans, and blend again. Add to the bowl, and stir both mixtures together until well mixed.

Pour into individual serving dishes, and sprinkle with a little cinnamon and sunflower seeds. Chill for several hours. If desired, top each with fresh fruit—mango, papaya, banana, strawberries, etc.—and a fresh mint leaf just before serving. Enjoy!

Note: Please avoid those pitted dried dates found in the supermarket. Buy plump, sweet, juicy medjool dates, generally found in the health food store or co-op.

4 cups water
1 cup whole wheat pastry flour
2 cups pitted medjool dates
1 cup pecans
Cinnamon and sunflower seeds, for garnish

Per serving: Calories 354, Protein 5 g, Fat 11 g, Carbohydrates 57 g

No-Cook Tofu Pudding

Yield: 4 servings

Who could ever eat "instant pudding" again after tasting this simple, delicious treat?

2 (12.3-ounce) packages extra-firm silken tofu
1 (8-ounce) jar fruit-sweetened jam, your choice of flavor*
1 ripe banana (optional)

*For a traditional Southwestern flavor, try prickly pear jelly.

Place all the ingredients in a blender, and pulse, stopping often to stir the ingredients with a long-handled wooden spoon or spatula. (Caution: Never stir anything in the blender while the motor is running.) Blend and stir until all the ingredients are mixed together well. Serve in an attractive dish, garnished, perhaps, with a little fresh fruit and a mint leaf. Enjoy!

VARIATIONS

For a great smoothie, substitute frozen fruit for the jam.

Pour the pudding into a pre-baked pie shell, and refrigerate to make a great cream pie. Garnish with fresh fruit and/or nuts.

Make different flavored puddings, and layer in a parfait glass. Top with nut pieces or fresh fruit.

Per serving: Calories 223, Protein 12 g, Fat 5 g, Carbohydrates 34 g

Rice Pudding

Yield: 4 servings

2 cups cooked brown rice
1 cup soymilk or rice milk
½ cup liquid sweetener
1 teaspoon cinnamon
½ cup raisins or currants
½ cup chopped fresh fruit, such as mangoes, peaches, apples, bananas, etc. (optional)
½ cup chopped nuts

Preheat the oven to 375°F.

Mix all the ingredients together, and place in an oiled baking dish. Cover and bake for about 40 to 45 minutes. Uncover and bake another 10 minutes.

Serve topped with a little soymilk or rice milk.

Per serving: Calories 424, Protein 6 g, Fat 9 g, Carbohydrates 77 g

Carob Fudge Brownies Muy Rica

Yield: nine 3-inch squares

A better-for-you version of the rich brownies we used to crave when the munchies hit.

Preheat the oven to 350°F.

In a large bowl, combine the flour, granulated sweetener, carob powder, and baking powder. Mix in the nuts and carob chips.

In a small bowl, mix the oil, maple syrup, egg replacer, and vanilla together. Add the liquid ingredients to the dry ingredients, and mix well, adding enough soymilk or rice milk to make a medium-thick batter. Pour into an oiled 9 x 9-inch pan. Bake for 25 minutes, or until a toothpick inserted in the center comes out clean. Cool in the pan and cut into nine squares. Serve and enjoy!

VARIATIONS

Add ½ cup raisins or currants.

For some interesting changes, add ¼ cup grain beverage (Pero, Inka, etc.) to the dry ingredients or, perhaps, a couple of tablespoons of peanut or cashew butter to the wet ingredients.

Dry ingredients:
2 cups whole wheat pastry flour
1 cup granulated sweetener
¼ cup carob powder
1 tablespoon baking powder
½ cup chopped nuts
½ cup carob chips

Liquid ingredients:
½ cup cold-pressed canola oil
¼ cup maple syrup, sorghum, or
  unsulfured molasses
Egg replacer equivalent to 2 eggs,
  p. 24
1 teaspoon pure vanilla
Soymilk or rice milk, as needed to
  thin the batter

Per square: Calories 389, Protein 6 g, Fat 17 g, Carbohydrates 51 g

Carrot Cake

Yield: 6 to 8 servings (one 4 x 8-inch loaf)

Here's a delicious, low-cal Carrot Cake with real taste satisfaction.

1½ cups whole wheat or spelt flour
½ teaspoon baking soda
½ teaspoon ground cinnamon
½ cup grated carrots
2 tablespoons chopped, toasted walnuts
5 tablespoons finely chopped fresh pineapple

4 egg whites, or egg replacer equivalent to 2 eggs, p. 24
2 tablespoons cold-pressed canola oil
3 tablespoons nonfat yogurt or soy yogurt
⅓ cup granulated or liquid sweetener
½ teaspoon pure vanilla

Preheat the oven to 325°F.

In a large mixing bowl, combine the flour, baking soda, and cinnamon. Add the carrots, pineapple, and walnuts, and mix thoroughly.

In another bowl, mix the egg whites or egg replacer, oil, yogurt, sweetener, and vanilla.

Pour the wet mixture into the dry. Mix well but do not beat. The batter should be light. If it's too heavy or dry, add a little more yogurt.

Pour into an oiled, 4 x 8-inch bread pan, and bake for 30 to 35 minutes, or until a toothpick inserted in the center comes out clean and dry. Cool and ice, if desired, with the following cream cheese frosting. Serve and enjoy!

VARIATIONS

For zucchini cake, substitute grated zucchini for the carrots. Substitute softened raisins or grated apple for the pineapple. A pinch of nutmeg or allspice will give it more of a spice cake flavor.

Per serving: Calories 189, Protein 6 g, Fat 5 g, Carbohydrates 29 g

CREAM CHEESE FROSTING

Yield: 1⅓ cups

1 cup dairy or soy cream cheese
⅓ cup granulated or liquid sweetener
½ teaspoon vanilla extract

Blend all the ingredients together very well.

VARIATIONS

For a richer flavor (but more fat), add 1 tablespoon softened butter or margarine to the frosting.

Add shredded, toasted coconut and/or ground pecans or walnuts for something different.

Per tablespoon: Calories 63, Protein 1 g, Fat 4 g, Carbohydrates 3 g

Gingerbread

Yield: nine 3-inch squares

Gingerbread or cake is a common dessert in the Southwest. This is sort of a cross between a brownie and cake, and delicious either way. Try it topped with the Banana-Pecan Sauce, page 176.

Preheat the oven to 350°F.

In a large bowl, beat together the molasses and oil. Add the boiling water.

In another bowl, mix all the dry ingredients together well, and add to the molasses mixture. Pour the batter (it will seem quite thin) into an oiled 9 x 9-inch pan, and bake for 40 minutes, or until a toothpick inserted in the middle comes out clean. Cool in the pan and cut into nine squares. Serve plain or with Banana-Pecan Sauce, page 176. Enjoy!

1 cup sorghum or unsulfured molasses
½ cup canola oil
½ cup boiling water

Dry ingredients:
1¼ cups whole wheat pastry flour
1 tablespoon baking powder
¼ teaspoon baking soda
Egg replacer equivalent to 1 egg, p. 24
1 teaspoon ground ginger
½ teaspoon ground cinnamon
¼ teaspoon nutmeg

Per square: Calories 292, Protein 3 g, Fat 12 g, Carbohydrates 42 g

Baked Stuffed Apples

Yield: 6 servings

People don't normally think of apples as Southwestern, but Wilcox, Arizona, grows some mighty tasty varieties. This makes a wonderfully light dessert, or try them for breakfast.

6 whole, large apples
½ cup peanut, cashew, or almond
 butter
¼ cup raisins or currants
¼ cup frozen apple juice
 concentrate or maple syrup
Dash of cinnamon

Preheat the oven to 350°F.

Leave the apples whole and unpeeled, but cut out the core. (You can buy special tools for coring apples or just carefully use a paring knife.)

In a small bowl, blend together the nut butter, sweetener, cinnamon, and raisins. Spoon this mixture into the center of the apples. Place the stuffed apples upright in a baking dish filled with about 1 inch of water. Bake about 1 hour, or until soft and cooked throughout. Serve hot and enjoy!

VARIATIONS

Add a few chopped nuts to the stuffing mixture. Perhaps add a pinch of nutmeg, cloves, or allspice. Chop some fresh fruit—peaches, apricots, pears, etc.—and mix into the stuffing.

Per serving: Calories 272, Protein 7 g, Fat 10 g, Carbohydrates 39 g

Banana-Pecan Sauce

Yield: 6 to 8 servings

Southern Arizona boasts some fine pecan orchards. This is also tasty over nondairy ice cream.

½ cup chopped raw pecans
¼ cup canola oil, butter, or
 margarine
2 ripe bananas, sliced or chopped
½ cup sorghum or unsulfured
 molasses

In a medium-sized heavy, dry skillet, lightly toast the pecans. Add the oil, bananas, and molasses, and cook over low heat another 5 minutes, or until heated throughout. Enjoy!

Per serving: Calories 232, Protein 1 g, Fat 13 g, Carbohydrates 29 g

Broiled Pineapple Rings

Yield: about 8 servings

There is absolutely no relationship between a ripe, fresh pineapple and the canned stuff they try to pass off on the unwitting consumer as pineapple. Here's a beautifully light and simple way to enjoy this tropical delicacy.

Preheat the oven to broil.

Arrange the pineapple rings on a baking sheet. Lightly drizzle with the maple syrup and just a pinch of cinnamon. Broil 5 to 7 minutes, or until the pineapple is lightly browned. Serve with a fresh mint sprig. Enjoy!

Note: This works well on a barbecue grill also.

1 ripe, fresh pineapple, peeled and sliced into 1-inch rings
¼ cup pure maple syrup
Pinch of cinnamon or ground ginger
Fresh mint leaves, for garnish

Per serving: Calories 83, Protein 0 g, Fat 0 g, Carbohydrates 19 g

Bunuelos

Yield: 4 servings

These tasty desserts or treats are best made just before serving. They are very simple to prepare but are decidedly not low-fat.

Fry the tortillas in hot oil until browned and crispy. Sprinkle with the sweetener or cinnamon, and serve hot or cold. Enjoy!

4 whole wheat tortillas
Canola oil for deep frying
1 tablespoon granulated sweetener
1 teaspoon cinnamon

Per serving: Calories 91, Protein 2 g, Fat 2 g, Carbohydrates 17 g

Fried Plantains or Bananas
Plantanos Fritos

Yield: 8 servings

While lower in calories than most desserts, I wouldn't call this delicious dessert low-calorie. Save it for special occasions. I like the plantains better than the bananas.

4 ripe, firm plantains or large
    bananas
2 tablespoons oil
2 tablespoons raw honey, brown
    rice syrup, or date sugar
Pinch of nutmeg
Cold-pressed canola oil for frying
1 tablespoon rum (optional)

Peel the plantains or bananas, and cut in ½-inch slices. Heat the oil in a heavy skillet over medium-high heat. Fry about 5 or 6 slices at a time. When golden brown on the bottom, turn and flatten a little with the spatula. Fry until brown and remove to a plate. Drizzle with the honey, brown rice syrup, and/or date sugar, and nutmeg. If you like, add the rum to the skillet with the oil. If you need to add more oil, do so but go lightly. Serve hot, perhaps with a nonfat frozen yogurt or a nondairy frozen dessert. Enjoy!

VARIATIONS

Preheat the oven to 350°F. Place the fried plantains in a baking dish, and drizzle with honey, brown rice syrup, or date sugar, and nutmeg, as above, but then sprinkle with a little unsweetened coconut. Bake about 15 to 20 minutes, or until hot and the coconut becomes toasted.

Per serving: Calories 155, Protein 1 g, Fat 3 g, Carbohydrates 30 g

Lemon Sherbet

Yield: 4 servings

Sweet and dairy-free, this light frozen dessert is the perfect ending to a special meal.

Combine everything except the lemon peel in a blender until smooth. Add the lemon peel, pour into a shallow pan, and place in the freezer. Stir every 20 minutes until frozen almost solid, about 1 hour. Spoon into individual serving dishes, and garnish with a mint leaf and a lemon wedge. Serve and enjoy!

1 (12.3-ounce) package soft silken tofu
2 tablespoons soymilk
⅓ cup raw honey or brown rice syrup
Juice of 2 lemons
1 teaspoon grated lemon peel

VARIATIONS

Try plain or lemon low-fat or nonfat yogurt in place of the tofu and soymilk.

Substitute lime juice or orange juice in place of lemon juice to make Lime Sherbet or Orange Sherbet.

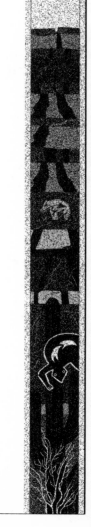

Per serving: Calories 134, Protein 4 g, Fat 3 g, Carbohydrates 23 g

Pecan Brittle

Yield: about 1 pound (30 pieces)

Every year when the pecans are harvested in St. David, Arizona, I like to buy a nice big bag and sit and shell them for pies and brittles. This recipe came about when I substituted pecans for the cashews in one of my favorite recipes. This is a little more chewy than "brittle," but it's still wonderful however you describe it. I must confess that I like the flavor of the organic butter better than the margarine. (I've not been able to make this come out with oil.)

¾ cup raw honey

¼ cup water

1 cup whole or chopped raw pecans

1 tablespoon organic butter or soy margarine

½ teaspoon pure vanilla

1 teaspoon baking soda

In a heavy, cast-iron skillet, boil the water and honey until it either reaches the soft ball mark on a candy thermometer or a small amount forms a soft ball when dropped into a bowl of ice water. Add the nuts and continue to boil until they become golden brown, about 10 to 12 minutes, stirring continuously.

Remove the skillet from the heat, and add the butter or margarine, vanilla, and baking soda. Mix well and pour the mixture onto an oiled cookie sheet. Refrigerate. When cool, break the candy into pieces. Serve and enjoy!

VARIATIONS

Substitute peanuts, cashews, almonds, sesame seeds, and/or unsweetened flake coconut for the pecans.

Lead me not into temptation; I can find the way myself.

—Rita Mae Brown

Per piece: Calories 55, Protein 0 g, Fat 3 g, Carbohydrates 8 g

DRINKS

Almond Date Shake

Yield: 4 servings

Use medjool or honey dates, rather than the dried dates you find in the produce department of the supermarket. There are some wonderful medjool dates grown in Northern Arizona.

3 cups milk or nondairy milk
9 to 10 large pitted dates
3 tablespoons chopped almonds

Blend all the ingredients together well. Garnish with a dash of cinnamon or nutmeg. Enjoy!

Per serving: Calories 179, Protein 8 g, Fat 6 g, Carbohydrates 25 g

Carob-Peanut Butter-Banana Shake

Yield: 4 servings

You can do just one flavor, if you prefer, by increasing that ingredient and eliminating the others. This is a great shake, though, and you owe it to yourself to give it a try this way at least once.

6 tablespoons natural peanut butter
2 tablespoons carob powder
2 ripe bananas
2 cups milk or nondairy milk
1 cup crushed ice
1 teaspoon pure vanilla extract

Blend all the ingredients together well. Enjoy!

VARIATIONS

For a really rich shake, substitute frozen yogurt or nondairy frozen dessert for the milk and ice.

Freeze the bananas first for a different texture.

Per serving: Calories 260, Protein 12 g, Fat 12 g, Carbohydrates 26 g

Chunky Monkey Shake

Yield: 2 servings

This delicious vegan shake packs a lot of nutrition in rich carob-cashew-banana decadence. Try some of the simple variations also.

Combine all the ingredients in a blender until smooth and creamy. Serve garnished with a mint leaf, and enjoy!

Although cocoa is often used in Southwestern and Mexican dishes, I have substituted carob here as a more nutritious alternative. For more information, see Hot Mexican Carob Drink on page 185.

VARIATIONS

Add a scoop or two of nondairy frozen dessert. Try other fruit (fresh or frozen) in place of the carob—strawberries, raspberries, peaches, etc.

All right, I give up. You can, of course, substitute sweetened chocolate or cocoa in place of the carob, although I, for one, much prefer the rich, earthy flavor of a good carob (and I sure don't miss the caffeine, oxalic acid, and theobromine that chocolate contains).

2 cups soymilk or rice milk
2 ripe bananas*
4 tablespoons roasted cashews**
2 tablespoons roasted carob powder
 plus 2 tablespoons granulated
 sweetener, or ¼ cup malt-
 sweetened carob chips

*I usually buy bananas 4 or 5 at a time, and, generally, 1 or 2 of them become very ripe before I have a chance to eat them. I put those very ripe bananas in the freezer, peel intact, and save them for banana bread or smoothies like this. Either thaw the banana and use it in your recipe or, in the case of smoothies, place the banana in a dish of hot water for about 30 seconds, or just until the peel becomes soft enough to remove. Use the rest of the banana frozen.

**It's very simple to roast raw cashews in a dry, heavy skillet (cast-iron works well) over medium heat, stirring often, until golden brown. These taste better than buying already-roasted cashews.

Per serving: Calories 365, Protein 9 g, Fat 13 g, Carbohydrates 52 g

Honey Lemonade or Limeade

Yield: 8 servings

When life gives you lemons, make lemonade.

—Unknown

Lemons and other citrus fruits are plentiful throughout most of the Southwest toward the end of winter. The honey adds a very nice flavor to the lemonade, better than just sweetening it with sugar. Try it also with brown rice syrup or even pure maple syrup.

1 cup of raw honey, or to taste

2 quarts cold water

Juice of 6 lemons

Juice of 2 limes

Juice of 1 orange (optional)

In a large pot, mix the honey and 2 cups of water, and cook slowly until the honey is completely dissolved. Add the rest of the water and the fruit juices, and mix well. Refrigerate or add ice cubes. (If the mixture is too hot, the ice will melt and the drink may become too weak.) Serve garnished with a lime slice and/or a sprig of mint. Enjoy!

VARIATION

Try with all lemons, all limes (use more; the limes are smaller), more oranges, or substitute grapefruit or tangerines.

Per serving: Calories 138, Protein 0 g, Fat 0 g, Carbohydrates 35 g

HIBISCUS TEA

Especially refreshing served over ice, hibiscus tea is available in natural foods stores. Steep as any tea and sweeten to taste with sweetener, if desired. Serve with a twist of lemon or lime.

Mango-Pineapple Shake

Yield: 4 servings

Blend all the ingredients together well. Enjoy!
Variations:

Soft tofu or soymilk with a little lemon juice will somewhat duplicate the cultured flavor of yogurt or buttermilk.

2 medium mangoes, pits removed and peeled
2 cups chopped fresh pineapple
3 cups yogurt, milk, or soymilk
Raw honey or brown rice syrup to sweeten (optional)
½ cup crushed ice (optional)

Per serving: Calories 211, Protein 12 g, Fat 0 g, Carbohydrates 39 g

Mexican Hot Carob Drink

Yield: 4 servings

Cocoa has been a traditional south-of-the-border beverage since the days of the Spanish conquistadors. For those wanting to avoid the caffeine or having an allergy to cocoa, carob makes a great substitute. Personally, I much prefer the flavor of a good quality carob to chocolate. The silken tofu in this drink makes it rich and creamy, just like a mug of hot cocoa, but tastier and more nutritious. Give it a try!

Blend the tofu and soymilk or rice milk in a blender until smooth. Place all the ingredients, except the vanilla and cinnamon sticks, in a large saucepan, and heat slowly just to the boiling point. Be careful not to boil. Reduce the heat and simmer for 2 minutes, stirring often. Stir in the vanilla and serve immediately garnished with a cinnamon stick. Enjoy!

1 (12.3-ounce) package soft silken tofu
2 cups soymilk or rice milk
⅓ cup roasted carob powder
½ cup granulated sweetener
¼ teaspoon ground cinnamon
Pinch of ground cloves (optional)
2 teaspoons coffee substitute or grain beverage
1 teaspoon pure vanilla
4 cinnamon sticks

Per serving: Calories 211, Protein 7 g, Fat 5 g, Carbohydrates 35 g

Orange Dream

Yield: 4 servings

½ cup frozen orange juice concentrate
2 cups milk or nondairy milk
½ cup powdered skim milk or soymilk
1 teaspoon pure vanilla extract
1 cup crushed ice

Blend all the ingredients together well. Garnish with a slice of orange. Enjoy!

VARIATIONS

Pineapple, apple, or other juice concentrate will work well in place of the orange juice concentrate.

If you like, add a little fresh pineapple.

Fresh fruit juice will work but will not have as strong a flavor as the juice concentrate. Fresh oranges will be too stringy in the blender.

Per serving: Calories 162, Protein 11 g, Fat 1 g, Carbohydrates 26 g

Orange Fizz

Yield: 4 servings

There's nothing like being able to walk out into your backyard and pick a handful of oranges for your morning juice. Yum!

2 cups orange juice
½ cup grapefruit juice
2 cups unflavored or orange-flavored carbonated mineral water

Whiz everything together well in the blender. Enjoy!

VARIATIONS

Try other juices and other fruits.

Per serving: Calories 110, Protein 1 g, Fat 0 g, Carbohydrates 26 g

Peach Fuzz

Yield: 4 servings

Blend all the ingredients together well. Garnish with a peach slice or a fresh sprig of mint. Enjoy!

VARIATIONS

Add a couple of sprigs of mint before blending. Fresh apricots substitute well for all or part of the peaches. Remember, it's your decision whether or not to peel the peaches.

2 to 3 peeled or unpeeled peaches, chopped
3 cups milk or nondairy milk
1 cup crushed ice

Per serving: Calories 131, Protein 7 g, Fat 2 g, Carbohydrates 21 g

Piña Colada Smoothie

Yield: 6 servings

Sip this refreshing drink with your eyes closed, and you'll almost feel the sea breezes of the Mexican coast.

Blend all the ingredients together well, and serve garnished with a mint leaf. Enjoy!

2 cups pineapple juice
2 cups coconut milk
1 cup raw honey or 1¼ cups granulated sweetener
2 cups soymilk or rice milk
1 teaspoon pure vanilla
2 cups crushed ice

Per serving: Calories 406, Protein 3 g, Fat 16 g, Carbohydrates 58 g

Purple Cow
or Purple Bean

Yield: 4 servings

This one is not actually blended, it's more of a float. But whatever you call it, it's delicious.

4 cups unsweetened organic grape
    juice

4 scoops frozen nonfat yogurt or
    nondairy frozen dessert

Place 1 cup of the juice in each of 4 glasses. Add a scoop of frozen dessert to each glass. Enjoy!

Per serving: Calories 205, Protein 3 g, Fat 1 g, Carbohydrates 46 g

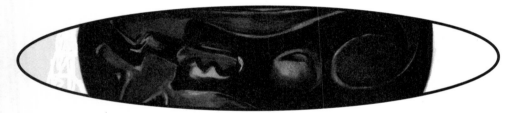

Roberto's Party Sangria

Yield: about 1 gallon

This refreshing party punch may be made with nonalcoholic wine. Float a few lime or orange slices in the punch bowl for a nice festive touch.

Juice of 3 to 4 lemons
Juice of 3 to 4 limes
Juice of 3 to 4 oranges
1 quart or liter red wine
1 quart white grape juice
1 quart or liter club soda or
    sparkling water

Mix all the ingredients together well, and serve over ice with a lime twist. Enjoy!

Per cup: Calories 99, Protein 1 g, Fat 0 g, Carbohydrates 14 g

Index

190

Ask your store to carry these books from the Healthy World Cuisine series, or you may order directly from:

The Book Publishing Company
P.O. Box 99
Summertown, TN 38483

A Taste Of Mexico 13.95
Delicious Jamaica. 11.95
Flavors Of India. 12.95
From A Traditional Greek Kitchen 12.95
From The Global Kitchen 11.95
From the Tables Of Lebanon. 12.95
Good Time Eatin' In Cajun Country 9.95
Indian Vegetarian Cooking at Your House. 12.95
Olive Oil Cookery (The Mediterranean Diet). 12.95

Or call: 1-800-695-2241
Please add $2.50 per book for shipping